THE

FOREST OF FIRE PEARLS ORACLE

THE MEDICINE WARRIOR I CHING

VOLUME III

RESEARCHES ON THE
TOLTEC I CHING

WILLIAM DOUGLAS HORDEN

3 + 4 :: 6 + 1 :: RETURN

ISBN-13:
978-1499565638

ISBN-10:
1499565631

DEDICATION

Master Khigh Alx Dhiegh
For his unstinting generosity of spirit

INTRODUCTION

This third volume of *Researches On The Toltec I Ching* is atavistic in that it reverts to the more primitive form of the original divinatory text, which consisted of mantic, or oracular, formulas with little or no commentary attached. In that vein, the oldest layers of the *Book Of Changes* furthered the oral tradition, making use of mnemonic aphorisms whose poetic-symbolic nature invoked the Oracle's message within the mind of the diviner. The title of this volume, *The Forest Of Fire Pearls Oracle*, comes from the ancient Chinese name for the traditional coin oracle method of consulting the *I Ching*.

The present volume can be consulted as a standalone divinatory text. It is, however, designed to be used in conjunction with *The Toltec I Ching*—as an adjunct to the material in that book, the present mantic formulas expand the range of interpretations open to the diviner. There are, beyond that, other features of this volume that recommend its study alongside *The Toltec I Ching*.

First, it places *The Toltec I Ching* hexagrams within the context of the older King Wen version. This it does by comparing both the individual hexagrams from each version, as well as the overall sequence of hexagrams from each version.

And, second, it provides mantic formulas for the *unchanging* lines in each hexagram. This is especially useful in analyzing a divination closely, since it is seldom the case that all six lines change in a reading. The Line Changes for a reading can, of course, be found in *The Toltec I Ching* hexagram texts, while the present volume provides a glimpse into the inertial, or unchanging, issues of the situation represented by the hexagram.

A brief note on nomenclature may be in order. There is no good word in English for the *gua* and *ba gua* (hexagram and trigram, respectively) of the *I Ching*. I have chosen to step away from trying to come up with a literal translation for these six- and three-lined figures, opting instead to use concepts that speak to the *experience* of those symbols. For this reason, I refer to the six-lined figures as *seasons* instead of hexagrams, in order to give a sense of the spatiality of each of the 64 archetypal situations: Just as we are immersed utterly in spring or summer, in other words, we occupy the season of Provoking Change or the season of Sensing Creation.

Likewise, I have chosen to use the word *nature* instead of trigram when referring to the three-lined figures. Specifically, this appears when describing the makeup of the *seasons*, which are composed of the *outer nature* and *inner nature* (rather than the upper trigram and lower trigram, respectively).

The subtitle of this volume, *The Medicine Warrior I Ching*, expands on the concept of the *spirit warrior*, which is developed fully in *The Toltec I Ching*. While the two terms are nearly synonymous, the *medicine warrior* places even more emphasis on the innate capacity of the individual to administer the appropriate *medicine*, or *benefit*, that restores balance to individuals or situations.

Regarding the organization of this volume, the text of each of the 64 Seasons is arranged in seven sections—

SECTION I: MANTIC FORMULA—three symbolic oracular statements epitomizing each Season, both summarizing and expanding on the lessons presented in *The Toltec I Ching*.

Sections II through IV express the relationship between the King Wen interpretation of the I Ching and *The Toltec I Ching*—

SECTION II: JUXTAPOSITION OF SEQUENCES—a side-by-side comparison of the hexagrams in the two sequences. It compares hexagram #1 in *The Toltec I Ching* to hexagram #1 in the King Wen version, followed, of course, by comparisons between hexagrams #2, hexagrams #3, and so on to hexagram #64 in their respective sequences.

SECTION III: EVOLUTION OF THE SEQUENCE—amends Section II, first making clear the trigram substitutions that lead from the King Wen to *The Toltec I Ching* hexagrams and, second, demonstrating the evolution of meaning as the King Wen hexagram "produces" its descendent in *The Toltec I Ching*.

SECTION IV: EVOLUTION OF THE HEXAGRAM—instead of their respective places in the sequence, this section focuses on the way that *The Toltec I Ching* hexagrams "resolve" their ancestral hexagrams in the King Wen version.

SECTION V: THE SEQUENCE OF SEASONS—this section clarifies the way in which each hexagram follows the previous one in *The Toltec I Ching* sequence.

SECTION VI: THE SOULS' JOURNEY—an archetypal development of the two souls (traditionally: the *hun* and *po*, the higher and lower souls, the immortal and mortal souls, respectively) on their pilgrimage in the Imaginal realm to complete the sacred work of transmutation.

SECTION VII: THE INERTIAL LINES—as mentioned above, interpretations for the *changing lines* already exist in *The Toltec I Ching*, which is why this section expresses (again, in the form of mantic formulas) the *unchanging lines*. In the course of a reading, the *changing lines* are those with values of 9 and 6, while the *unchanging lines* are those with values of 7 and 8 (see Appendix on the coin oracle method).

A NOTE ON INTERPRETING THE ORACLE

It has long been said that the more time diviners spend with the Oracle, the more their own minds come to mirror the Mind of the Oracle. This affinity is based on a deep resonance between the microcosm and the macrocosm, between the part and the Whole, between diviner and Oracle—a communion of shared presence that permeates the *field of possibilities* intersecting the *field of intentions*. Awareness that permeates this intersection is called *mystic intuition*.

Tempting as it is to establish definitive rules for interpreting the Oracle's reply to our questions, experience demonstrates that it is far more valuable to establish a relationship of *mystic intuition* with the Oracle.

In particular: It is true that generally when one hexagram changes into another, the first can be interpreted as the present and the second as the future developments—but it cannot be said that this is always the case. There are times that the first hexagram shows the result of taking one path and the second hexagram the results of taking a different path: This often shows up when people are consulting about a specific choice or decision and can be thought of as the Oracle saying, *This decision leads here and that decision leads there*.

Experience also shows that the more specific a question is, especially about material issues (like health and finances, for example), the more general the symbols used in the Oracle's reply. A question like, "What should I do about my health?" for instance, might generate a reply of #44 Refining Instinct changing into #35 Holding Back. The diviner might read through both texts and find little that seems to answer the question—but if *mystic intuition* serves, then the answer emerges from a straight-forward reading of the hexagram titles: *Refine the instinctual appetites (#44), make them more subtle-spiritual through self-restraint (#35)*.

It has long been observed of the Oracle that the emperor asking about whether to move the capital and the farmer asking about when to plant the fields might both receive exactly the same reply—and that the answer applies equally well to both. Such is the nature of symbol, which is the language of the Oracle: The symbol's meaning is directed by the nature of the question.

The best interpretations come when diviners develop and trust their *mystic intuition*.

The
Forest of Fire Pearls Oracle

The Medicine Warrior I Ching

SEASON 1
PROVOKING CHANGE

OUTER NATURE:	**LIGHTNING**
INNER NATURE:	**LIGHTNING**

I. MANTIC FORMULA

Lightning within, Lightning without: The season of PROVOKING CHANGE arrives. Success comes to those who are not unnerved by the unexpected.

Emulate the earthquake in every thought, word, and deed: The situation is one of transforming tensions in order to break through stagnation.

Create or perish: Long-lasting good fortune can be initiated by those who harness the elemental forces at work in the season of PROVOKING CHANGE.

II. JUXTAPOSITION OF SEQUENCES

Toltec I Ching Hexagram #1
Provoking Change

Upper Trigram: Lightning
Lower Trigram: Lightning

King Wen Hexagram #1
The Creative

Upper Trigram: Sun
Lower Trigram: Sun

III. EVOLUTION OF SEQUENCE

Lightning stands in the place of Sun above, Lightning stands in the place of Sun below: That which is the most purposive and creative is the capacity to beneficially provoke change.

IV. EVOLUTION OF HEXAGRAM

Hexagram #51 LIVING ESSENCE resolves the cosmological sky-force of THE CREATIVE by returning its generative energy to the animating and guiding force within all things. Sun facing Sun was dynamic strength upon dynamic strength in THE CREATIVE—but is transformed into creative potential upon creative potential in the season of *LIVING ESSENCE*.

V. THE SEQUENCE OF SEASONS

*Stirred to movement by the inevitable ending,
the true self begins the cycle of metamorphosis anew.*

*Before there is a beginning, something must initiate movement:
PROVOKING CHANGE is the unforeseen ending.*

VI. THE SOULS' JOURNEY

*Every path leads to an impasse and the guide has lost the way:
The traveler stops at last and begins to build the city.*

VII. THE INERTIAL LINES

Seven in the First Place:

*The stone that one first stumbles across is set aside
for the capstone of the work.*

Seemingly by accident, fate sets one's foot on the path to mastery.

Eight in the Second Place:

*False hopes, when properly tempered,
lead to true greatness.*

Unreachable goals are attained by the truly disciplined.

Eight in the Third Place:

*Injustice begets nobility,
corruption begets righteousness.*

One transmutes the base into the fine.

12

Seven in the Fourth Place:

The messengers bear no news of the outside world,
*   the soul travels the medicine road.*

The senses cannot say what kind of healer one is becoming.

Eight in the Fifth Place:

The ancestors' compass
*   guides one's footsteps.*

The lodestar of spirit has not changed position.

Eight in the Sixth Place:

One envisions one's work bearing fruit
*   elsewhere.*

One's contemporaries are not the only audience.

SEASON 2
SENSING CREATION

OUTER NATURE: **LAKE**
INNER NATURE: **LAKE**

I. MANTIC FORMULA

Lake within, Lake without: The season of SENSING CREATION arrives. Success comes to those who immerse themselves in the joy of life.

Reflect generosity in every thought, word, and deed: The situation is one in which a period of estrangement and misunderstanding gives way to a period of harmony and contentment.

Embody the living spirit of happiness: The soul envisions a home worth bequeathing to future generations in the season of SENSING CREATION.

II. JUXTAPOSITION OF SEQUENCES

Toltec I Ching Hexagram #2
Sensing Creation

King Wen Hexagram #2
The Receptive

Upper Trigram: Lake
Lower Trigram: Lake

Upper Trigram: Moon
Lower Trigram: Moon

III. EVOLUTION OF SEQUENCE

Lake stands in the place of Moon above, Lake stands in the place of Moon below: That which is the most open and receptive is the capacity to fully sense the miraculous nature of Creation.

14

IV. Evolution of Hexagram

Hexagram #58 DAWNING EXISTENCE resolves the cosmological earth-force of THE RECEPTIVE by returning its generative energy to the nurturing and sustaining force circulating among all things. Moon facing Moon was receptive devotion upon receptive devotion in THE RECEPTIVE—but is transformed into realizing potential upon realizing potential in the season of *DAWNING EXISTENCE.*

V. The Sequence Of Seasons

Hearts reawakened to wonder,
the true self welcomes all into the unconditional immersion of universal communion.

After things have been stirred to movement, they are at their most open:
SENSING CREATION is the awakening of unforeseen perceptions.

VI. The Souls' Journey

A cavern with an underground spring echoes with the voices of the ancestors:
The guide understands the ancient tongue, the traveler translates it into stone.

VII. The Inertial Lines

Seven in the First Place:

The threshold of the great mystery
is crossed at every union.

One light and one dark make a Way.

Seven in the Second Place:

At each new level,
the roles of hand and instrument reverse.

One is being well-used by life.

Eight in the Third Place:

The messengers bear news from the four winds,
the soul rides the fifth wind.

In the midst of the world, alone with the World Soul.

Seven in the Fourth Place:

> *No time is lost*
> > *between lives.*
>
> *A single purpose spans all one's lifetimes.*

Seven in the Fifth Place:

> *One walks backwards*
> > *from the future.*
>
> *Each landmark on the path is remembered ahead of time.*

Eight in the Sixth Place:

> *Wisdom is honed on the whetstone*
> > *of the sacredness of everything.*
>
> *The great-souled act like sacred beings among sacred beings.*

SEASON 3
RECOGNIZING ANCESTRY

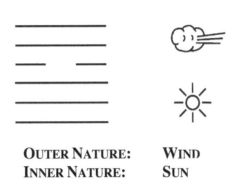

OUTER NATURE: **WIND**
INNER NATURE: **SUN**

I. MANTIC FORMULA

Sun within, Wind without: The season of RECOGNIZING ANCESTRY arrives. Success comes to those who identify with something greater than themselves.

You become what you name yourself: The situation is one of acknowledging the lineage to which you belong.

Personify the perfected face and perfected heart: The awakened immortality of the spirit body beckons to those who utter their secret name in the season of RECOGNIZING ANCESTRY.

II. JUXTAPOSITION OF SEQUENCES

Toltec I Ching Hexagram #3
Recognizing Ancestry

King Wen Hexagram #3
Difficulty In The Beginning

Upper Trigram: Wind
Lower Trigram: Sun

Upper Trigram: Water
Lower Trigram: Lightning

III. EVOLUTION OF SEQUENCE

Wind stands in the place of Water above, Sun stands in the place of Lightning below: That which sets out for the unknown destination aims for the primordial origin.

IV. Evolution of Hexagram

Hexagram #9 Uprooting Fear resolves the anxious caution of Difficulty in the Beginning by returning its generative energy to indomitable daring. Lightning facing Water was too cautious amid confusion in Difficulty in the Beginning—but is transformed into inspired courage in the face of uncertain risks in the season of *Uprooting Fear*.

V. The Sequence Of Seasons

Imprinted with the vision of original perfection,
the true self feels itself part of a spiritual lineage with an established role in the completion of creation.

After things have been imprinted, they are attuned to the same image:
Recognizing Ancestry *is the web of invisible threads binding the visible.*

VI. The Souls' Journey

The traveler knows nothing but the road, the guide knows nothing but the stars:
The world tree stands between them, marking the center of the world.

VII. The Inertial Lines

Seven in the First Place:

> *Those who honor their family tree*
> *   are surprised by the depth of its roots.*

> *The wisdom teachings one seeks are older than language.*

Seven in the Second Place:

> *Communities bound by living traditions*
> *   need no laws.*

> *The allies one seeks share meaningful everyday rituals.*

Seven in the Third Place:

> *Everything is anchored to the light*
> *   by its shadow.*

> *The wholeness one seeks can be experienced but not described.*

Eight in the Fourth Place:

Even time itself must kneel
*   before the seed within the ripened fruit.*

The circle one seeks to understand is knotted seamlessly.

Seven in the Fifth Place:

Everything exchanges lightning
*   forever, without interruption.*

The center one seeks is within.

Seven in the Sixth Place:

Thoughts are as far apart
*   as stars.*

The peace one seeks is between thoughts.

SEASON 4
MIRRORING WISDOM

OUTER NATURE:	**FIRE**
INNER NATURE:	**WIND**

I. MANTIC FORMULA

Wind within, Fire without: The season of MIRRORING WISDOM arrives. Success comes to all who satisfy their love of understanding.

Allow yourself to be taken captive by your wonder: The situation is one of steeping yourself in the knowledge and practices of those you most admire.

Polish the mirror: The medicine warrior is able to gaze unflinchingly upon the image cast by the smoking mirror of truth in the season of MIRRORING WISDOM.

II. JUXTAPOSITION OF SEQUENCES

Toltec I Ching Hexagram #4
Mirroring Wisdom

King Wen Hexagram #4
Youthful Folly

Upper Trigram: Fire
Lower Trigram: Wind

Upper Trigram: Mountain
Lower Trigram: Water

III. EVOLUTION OF SEQUENCE

Fire stands in the place of Mountain above, Wind stands in the place of Water below: That which requires tempering and seasoning finds it in the lessons and wisdom teachings of nature.

IV. EVOLUTION OF HEXAGRAM

Hexagram #50 NARROWING AIM resolves the naive inexperience of YOUTHFUL FOLLY by returning its generative energy to practiced mastery. Water facing the Mountain was too impetuous amid obstacles in YOUTHFUL FOLLY—but is transformed into unfathomable potential in the face of sustained stability in the season of *NARROWING AIM*.

V. THE SEQUENCE OF SEASONS

Walking the ancient path,
the true self seeks being over thinking.

After things are knotted together, they are untied:
MIRRORING WISDOM is the reflecting of the common origin.

VI. THE SOULS' JOURNEY

The guardians cry out from within the world tree:
The traveler may build here only if the umbilical cord is never cut.

VII. THE INERTIAL LINES

Eight in the First Place:

Coyotes call to one another
within the shadows of the sun's eclipse.

Untamed souls sense one another's presence in the great mystery.

Seven in the Second Place:

Two mirrors facing one another
reflect the gaze of spirit.

Savants reflect the awareness that is fully awake but not thinking.

Seven in the Third Place:

The pursuit of peace of mind
leads to discontent.

Savants simply accept the gift they cannot find by searching.

Seven in the Fourth Place:

> *The actor wears*
> > *a thousand masks.*

> *The true self is an open secret.*

Eight in the Fifth Place:

> *Distilling the wind,*
> > *one becomes medicine.*

> *The essence of the invisible is the panacea.*

Seven in the Sixth Place:

> *The ancestors' seeds of intent are carried*
> > *on the four winds.*

> *The dreams of the ancients inspire the world to act.*

SEASON 5
RESTORING WHOLENESS

OUTER NATURE: WIND
INNER NATURE: LIGHTNING

I. MANTIC FORMULA

Lightning within, Wind without: The season of RESTORING WHOLENESS arrives. Success comes to those who envision what needs to be returned to its original nature.

Do not amputate the phantom limb: The situation is one of being haunted by a growing awareness of something essential that has been lost, hidden, or forgotten.

Mimic the lizard's tail: The medicine warrior refrains from expending energy on anything but the act of healing in the season of RESTORING WHOLENESS.

II. JUXTAPOSITION OF SEQUENCES

Toltec I Ching Hexagram #5
Restoring Wholeness

Upper Trigram: Wind
Lower Trigram: Lightning

King Wen Hexagram #5
Waiting

Upper Trigram: Water
Lower Trigram: Sun

III. EVOLUTION OF SEQUENCE

Wind stands in the place of Water above, Lightning stands in the place of Sun below: That which waits patiently for the right time finds itself restored to wholeness.

IV. Evolution of Hexagram

Hexagram #42 INTERPRETING INSIGHT resolves the patient prudence of WAITING by returning its generative energy to conscientious self-expression. Sun facing Water was strength holding itself in check amid uncertainty in WAITING—but is transformed into creative power in the face of unfathomable mystery in the season of *INTERPRETING INSIGHT*.

V. The Sequence Of Seasons

The wisdom teachings show the true self
the way to call back lost parts of wholeness.

After things have revealed the beginning, they embody the destination:
RESTORING WHOLENESS is the growing back of what had been lost.

VI. The Souls' Journey

A thunderbolt blasts the world tree:
The guardians are released back into the world.

VII. The Inertial Lines

Seven in the First Place:

One lures the wounded
into the net of medicine.

The great-souled target benefit to specific need.

Eight in the Second Place:

Wholeness can be postponed
but not evaded.

The inevitability of perfection spans lifetimes.

Eight in the Third Place:

The heart of the mountain
echoes one's call.

The cavern of hidden treasures beckons.

24

Eight in the Fourth Place:

Success breeds envy,
acclaim breeds slander.

Savants forget ills by praising all.

Seven in the Fifth Place:

Teachers and students avoid
the pit of understanding.

Knowing is the tip of the iceberg of living truth.

Seven in the Sixth Place:

Self-sacrifice moves
the sun and moon.

Willingly giving up the ego identity frees the true self.

SEASON 6
FOSTERING SELF-SACRIFICE

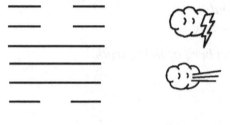

OUTER NATURE:	LIGHTNING
INNER NATURE:	WIND

I. MANTIC FORMULA

Wind within, Lightning without: The season of FOSTERING SELF-SACRIFICE arrives. Success comes to those who wait for the next opportunity.

Beware the web of silk and gold: The situation is one of benefiting others instead of attempting to advance a just cause at the wrong time.

Stay true to your compass heading: The soul practices patience and discernment in the season of FOSTERING SELF-SACRIFICE.

II. JUXTAPOSITION OF SEQUENCES

Toltec I Ching Hexagram #6
Fostering Self-Sacrifice

King Wen Hexagram #6
Conflict

Upper Trigram: Lightning
Lower Trigram: Wind

Upper Trigram: Sun
Lower Trigram: Water

III. EVOLUTION OF SEQUENCE

Lightning stands in the place of Sun above, Wind stands in the place of Water below: That which begets conflict fosters self-sacrifice.

IV. Evolution of Hexagram

Hexagram #32 CONTROLLING CONFRONTATION resolves the inherent discord of CONFLICT by returning its generative energy to farsighted self-restraint. Water facing Sun was ulterior motives with too much strength in CONFLICT—but is transformed into recognizing the unconscious in the face of great power in the season of *CONTROLLING CONFRONTATION*.

V. The Sequence Of Seasons

In the midst of resurgent possibilities,
the true self identifies with the whole, sacrificing short-term gain for long-term good fortune.

After things have been revitalized, they are at their most prolific:
FOSTERING SELF-SACRIFICE is the continuation of one's fortunes.

VI. The Souls' Journey

The sap of the world tree runs out upon the ground:
The trunk may be broken but the roots live on.

VII. The Inertial Lines

Eight in the First Place:

The ancestors send dreams
to awaken the medicine body.

Spiritual allies guide the open-hearted.

Seven in the Second Place:

The conquered
conquer the conquerors.

Indomitable spirit holds the moral high ground.

Seven in the Third Place:

Goats butt heads,
opossums play dead.

Everyone speaks their own language.

Seven in the Fourth Place:

> *One advances*
> > *without moving.*

> *Striving is not as advantageous as effortlessness.*

Eight in the Fifth Place:

> *In times of ignorance,*
> > *the work must be disguised.*

> *Where fear rules, free-thinking must act wisely.*

Eight in the Sixth Place:

> *One dwells*
> > *on the road of stillness.*

> *Thought has no fixed abode but contentment.*

SEASON 7
COMPELLING MOTIVE

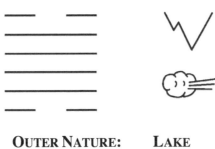

OUTER NATURE: LAKE
INNER NATURE: WIND

I MANTIC FORMULAS

Wind within, Lake without: The season of COMPELLING MOTIVE arrives. Success comes to those who willingly sacrifice comfort and routine in order to pursue their ruling passion.

Do not tarry at the crossroads: The situation is one of coming to a momentous decision.

Listen to the past, speak to the future: The soul is possessed by the sense of spiritual duty in the season of COMPELLING MOTIVE.

II. JUXTAPOSITION OF SEQUENCES

Toltec I Ching Hexagram #7
Compelling Motive

Upper Trigram: Lake
Lower Trigram: Wind

King Wen Hexagram #7
The Army

Upper Trigram: Moon
Lower Trigram: Water

III. EVOLUTION OF SEQUENCE

Lake stands in the place of Moon above, Wind stands in the place of Water below: That which seeks to mobilize people finds a compelling motive.

IV. Evolution of Hexagram

Hexagram #28 Synchronizing Movement resolves the martial organization of The Army by returning its generative energy to spontaneous coordination. Water facing Moon was human resources to be marshaled in The Army — but is transformed into unfathomable mystery in the face of cyclic ripenings in the season of *Synchronizing Movement*.

V. The Sequence Of Seasons

Passing through a time of upheaval,
the true self awakens a passion that will not be denied.

After things are dedicated to the end, they are at their most vulnerable:
Compelling Motive is the protection of the seed.

VI. The Souls' Journey

The world tree is hewn and fashioned into four gates:
They open, they close, to the guardians' password alone.

VII. The Inertial Lines

Eight in the First Place:

The forces of the world are compelled
to safeguard even the least spark of the divine fire.

One identifies with indestructible essence.

Seven in the Second Place:

Light, love and laughter
answer one's call.

One's intent is blessed.

Seven in the Third Place:

The delight of the senses
fans the flame of the divine.

There is no shadow where all is light.

Seven in the Fourth Place:

Everything awaits the opportunity
to surprise itself.

The new ever springs from the unknown.

Seven in the Fifth Place:

The forbidden fruit hangs on the branch
next to the hornet's nest.

Excitement too easily makes unexpected turns.

Eight in the Sixth Place:

If there is no escape,
it is not a trap.

Destinations are not always recognized immediately.

SEASON 8
HARMONIZING DUALITY

OUTER NATURE: **WIND**
INNER NATURE: **LAKE**

I. MANTIC FORMULA

Lake within, Wind without: The season of HARMONIZING DUALITY arrives. Success comes to those who balance the furthest extremes.

You speak with your own voice: The situation is one of consciously unifying one's dual nature.

Make offerings and pilgrimages: One lives as if one had invented living in the season of HARMONIZING DUALITY.

II. JUXTAPOSITION OF SEQUENCES

Toltec I Ching Hexagram #8
Harmonizing Duality

King Wen Hexagram #8
Holding Together [Union]

Upper Trigram: Wind
Lower Trigram: Lake

Upper Trigram: Water
Lower Trigram: Moon

III. EVOLUTION OF SEQUENCE

Wind stands in the place of Water above, Lake stands in the place of Moon below: That which desires to bind people together finds the way to harmonize the polarities among them.

32

IV. Evolution of Hexagram

Hexagram #61 STRENGTHENING INTEGRITY resolves the central authority of HOLDING TOGETHER by returning its generative energy to mutual reverence. Moon facing Water was voluntary submission to charismatic authority in HOLDING TOGETHER—but is transformed into mutual reflection in the face of unfathomable mystery in the season of *STRENGTHENING INTEGRITY*.

V. The Sequence Of Seasons

Whole-heartedly pursuing personal purpose,
the true self is attuned to the universal intent.

After things are driven to preserve the beginning, they find their true worth:
HARMONIZING DUALITY is the acceptance of the immutable.

VI. The Souls' Journey

The traveler and the guide are possessed by the same homesickness:
Before the first stone is laid, the city already stands immortal.

VII. The Inertial Lines

Seven in the First Place:

The space between things
is always deeper than it is wide.

The invisible differences draw things together.

Seven in the Second Place:

The ripening of this season's fruit
gives birth to next year's seedling.

Savants welcome the completion of another cycle.

Eight in the Third Place:

Nothing changes
but the mind.

The changing within the unchanging is the source of confusion.

Eight in the Fourth Place:

> *Everything changes*
> > *but mind.*

> *The unchanging within the changing is the source of well-being.*

Seven in the Fifth Place:

> *Fearing the cocoon,*
> > *caterpillars cannot recognize butterflies.*

> *The window of metamorphosis opens onto two different worlds.*

Seven in the Sixth Place:

> *The leap*
> > *is the landing.*

> *The spirit body enters the formless.*

SEASON 9
UPROOTING FEAR

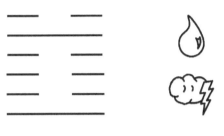

OUTER NATURE: **WATER**
INNER NATURE: **LIGHTNING**

I. MANTIC FORMULA

Lightning within, Water without: The season of UPROOTING FEAR arrives. Success comes to those who dare to act with abandon.

You discover what is worth fighting for: The situation is one in which something pernicious has taken root and threatens to overrun that which is most worth preserving.

Overcome or be overcome: Righteous creativity arises not from the wrongs done to oneself but from the wrongs done to others in the season of UPROOTING FEAR.

II. JUXTAPOSITION OF SEQUENCES

Toltec I Ching Hexagram #9
Uprooting Fear

Upper Trigram: Water
Lower Trigram: Lightning

King Wen Hexagram #9
The Taming Power of the Small

Upper Trigram: Wind
Lower Trigram: Sun

III. EVOLUTION OF SEQUENCE

Water stands in the place of Wind above, Lightning stands in the place of Sun below: That which moderates the stronger enters each encounter without fear of loss.

IV. Evolution of Hexagram

Hexagram #3 Recognizing Ancestry resolves the petty tyranny of THE TAMING POWER OF THE SMALL by returning its generative energy to spiritual homecoming. Sun facing Wind was strength being held in check by indirect manipulation in THE TAMING POWER OF THE GREAT — but is transformed into initiation in the face of unfathomable mystery in the season of *RECOGNIZING ANCESTRY*.

V. The Sequence Of Seasons

Finding immortality in the indivisible,
the true self advances without trepidation.

After things have discovered the real, they must contend with the unreal:
UPROOTING FEAR is the eradication of illusion.

VI. The Souls' Journey

The ground is overgrown with weeds and filled with rocks:
Before the city can be built, a place must be cleared.

VII. The Inertial Lines

Seven in the First Place:

Self-deception requires more mental discipline
than self-acceptance.

People who are already happy find one another.

Eight in the Second Place:

The endeavor flourishes with shared tasks,
not talk.

Concrete actions outshine abstract goals.

Eight in the Third Place:

Those drinking from the mirage do not know the thirst
of those who return to the oasis.

The bliss of communion remains a mystery to troubled spirits.

Eight in the Fourth Place:

One is sought for one's character,
*   not one's achievements.*

Savants look for the purities of mind.

Seven in the Fifth Place:

The exchange of divine sustenance for human metamorphosis
*   is the mortar of the fortress of community.*

Absolute sincerity transcends self-interest.

Eight in the Sixth Place:

One serpent,
*   many sheddings.*

Each lifetime is wood for the bonfire of immortality.

SEASON 10
UNIFYING INSPIRATION

| OUTER NATURE: | LIGHTNING |
| INNER NATURE: | MOON |

I. MANTIC FORMULA

Moon within, Lightning without: The season of UNIFYING INSPIRATION arrives. Success comes to those whose vision is reflected in the hearts of many.

You embody the soul's spirit: The situation is one of embodying the alternative to escalating discord and renewed conflict.

Your thoughts attract butterflies: One's mind flowers from the soil of life but is pollinated within the realm of spirit during the season of UNIFYING INSPIRATION.

II. JUXTAPOSITION OF SEQUENCES

| Toltec I Ching Hexagram #10 | King Wen Hexagram #10 |
| Unifying Inspiration | Treading [Conduct] |

Upper Trigram: Lightning   Upper Trigram: Sun
Lower Trigram: Moon   Lower Trigram: Lake

III. EVOLUTION OF SEQUENCE

Lightning stands in the place of Sun above, Moon stands in the place of Lake below: That which strives for ethical behavior between weak and strong finds an unifying inspiration.

IV. EVOLUTION OF HEXAGRAM

Hexagram #16 RENEWING DEVOTION resolves the accepted inequality of TREADING by returning its generative energy to the shared birthright. Lake facing Sun was innocence amid great power in TREADING—but is transformed into awe in the face of creation in the season of *RENEWING DEVOTION*.

V. THE SEQUENCE OF SEASONS

The true self transforms self-confidence
into faith in a common vision.

After things are cleared, they are charged with a new movement:
UNIFYING INSPIRATION is the impassioning of the will.

VI. THE SOULS' JOURNEY

The sacred mountain moves, circling the city:
Every stone of every monument and road must be quarried from the mountain's spirit.

VII. THE INERTIAL LINES

Eight in the First Place:

Doomsaying is a tactic
of desperation.

Crying infants need attention.

Eight in the Second Place:

Constant novelty is a tactic
of distraction.

Those unable to concentrate make uneasy allies.

Eight in the Third Place:

Elitism is a tactic
of enslavement.

Savants forge an alliance outside the walls.

Seven in the Fourth Place:

> *Courage is a tactic*
> *of compassion.*
>
> *Caring for others in need drives one to action.*

Eight in the Fifth Place:

> *Rejoicing is a tactic*
> *of liberation.*
>
> *The chains of unease cannot bind the ecstatic spirit.*

Eight in the Sixth Place:

> *Secrecy is a tactic*
> *of accomplishment.*
>
> *The great-souled shroud their greatest acts in anonymity.*

SEASON 11
ATTRACTING ALLIES

OUTER NATURE: LAKE
INNER NATURE: LIGHTNING

I. MANTIC FORMULA

Lightning within, Lake without: The season of ATTRACTING ALLIES arrives. Success comes to those whose thoughts, words, and deeds precisely mirror one another.

Make yourself worthy of the noblest allies: The situation is one in which one cannot possibly succeed alone.

Wait to be approached by those you admire: The soul's only motive is to respond with the utmost integrity to each moment in the season of ATTRACTING ALLIES.

II. JUXTAPOSITION OF SEQUENCES

Toltec I Ching Hexagram #11
Attracting Allies

King Wen Hexagram #11
Peace

Upper Trigram: Lake
Lower Trigram: Lightning

Upper Trigram: Moon
Lower Trigram: Sun

III. EVOLUTION OF SEQUENCE

Lake stands in the place of Moon above, Lightning stands in the place of Sun below: That which seeks peace attracts allies.

IV. Evolution of Hexagram

Hexagram #17 Guiding Force resolves the social harmony of PEACE by returning its generative energy to perpetual transformation. Sun facing Moon was strength voluntarily subordinating itself to complementary nurturance in PEACE—but is transformed into primordial beginnings in the face of cyclic endings in the season of *GUIDING FORCE*.

V. The Sequence Of Seasons

Embodying the common good,
the true self draws collaborators from afar.

After things have momentum, they become apparent elsewhere:
ATTRACTING ALLIES is the spontaneous echoing of hearts.

VI. The Souls' Journey

An earthquake blesses the work:
The guardians raise the city's walls.

VII. The Inertial Lines

Seven in the First Place:

The plow horse, not the racehorse,
claims the prize.

The time arrives for conscientious sustained effort.

Eight in the Second Place:

At the crossroads of fire and water,
the living medicine flashes and thunders.
Opposites unite in new opportunities to heal.

Eight in the Third Place:

The unified heart
finds no faults.

The clearer the eyes, the purer the world.

Seven in the Fourth Place:

Better to describe wisdom
than to advise against folly.

Inspiration, not admonishment, spurs change.

Seven in the Fifth Place:

The wise find truth
in the lie of mortality.

One allies oneself with the great-souled ones of all time.

Eight in the Sixth Place:

An ancient light reappears,
eclipsing sun, moon, and stars.

The inner sky is illumined by the act of creation.

SEASON 12
SEEING AHEAD

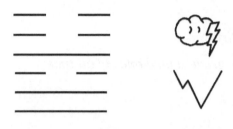

OUTER NATURE: **LIGHTNING**
INNER NATURE: **LAKE**

I. MANTIC FORMULA

Lake within, Lightning without: The season of SEEING AHEAD arrives. Success comes to those who sense the rhythm of change.

You see the way forward: The situation is one of mapping out a concrete plan for the future.

Things are conceived three seasons before they are born: Long before matters cross the threshold of change, the seeds of emerging circumstances can be discerned in the season of SEEING AHEAD.

II. JUXTAPOSITION OF SEQUENCES

Toltec I Ching Hexagram #12
Seeing Ahead

Upper Trigram: Lightning
Lower Trigram: Lake

King Wen Hexagram #12
Standstill [Stagnation]

Upper Trigram: Sun
Lower Trigram: Moon

III. EVOLUTION OF SEQUENCE

Lightning stands in the place of Sun above, Lake stands in the place of Moon below: That which avoids falling into stagnation sees ahead.

IV. EVOLUTION OF HEXAGRAM

Hexagram #54 Repeating Test resolves the stagnating separation of STANDSTILL by returning its generative energy to correcting history. Moon facing Sun was nurturance withdrawing from strong action in STANDSTILL—but is transformed into reflective awareness in the face of new beginnings in the season of *REPEATING TEST*.

V. THE SEQUENCE OF SEASONS

Familiarity with the field of action gives the true self
a keen perspective on developing trends.

After things have been conjoined, they have altered the future:
SEEING AHEAD is the throwing forward of sight.

VI. THE SOULS' JOURNEY

In the mouth of the cave, a campfire burns all night:
The guardians recount their dreams, the guide remembers the way again.

VII. THE INERTIAL LINES

Seven in the First Place:

Hope and fear
    cloud the vision.

Savants break through to unpredictability.

Seven in the Second Place:

Praise and censure,
    dust and cobwebs.

Savants create and move on, create and move on.

Eight in the Third Place:

The loom cannot prevent the hand
    from making inspired mistakes.

Random spontaneity is essential to the art of living.

Seven in the Fourth Place:

Tears are better teachers
than claws and fangs.

Displays of vulnerability civilize people.

Eight in the Fifth Place:

The future calls,
the past echoes.

One holds to living visions even as others hold to dying visions.

Eight in the Sixth Place:

The kite sails free
when its string breaks.

Accident, coincidence, decision and fate are all one .

SEASON 13
CONCENTRATING ATTENTION

OUTER NATURE:	LIGHTNING
INNER NATURE:	MOUNTAIN

I. MANTIC FORMULA

Mountain within, Lightning without: The season of CONCENTRATING ATTENTION arrives. Success comes to those who are not distracted by their objective.

Your aim, arrow, and target are all one and the same: The situation is one of single-minded presence.

The opossum travels with her young in her pouch: The medicine warrior ennobles the destination by ennobling each step of the way in the season of CONCENTRATING ATTENTION.

II. JUXTAPOSITION OF SEQUENCES

Toltec I Ching Hexagram #13
Concentrating Attention

King Wen Hexagram #13
Fellowship with Men

Upper Trigram: Lightning
Lower Trigram: Mountain

Upper Trigram: Sun
Lower Trigram: Fire

III. EVOLUTION OF SEQUENCE

Lightning stands in the place of Sun above, Mountain stands in the place of Fire below: That which unites people in true fellowship embodies a sincerity that is the unbroken focus of attention.

47

IV. Evolution of Hexagram

Hexagram #62 Conceiving Spirit resolves the ennobling purpose of FELLOWSHIP WITH MEN by returning its generative energy to spiritual light. Fire facing Sun was discernment with strength in FELLOWSHIP WITH MEN—but is transformed into first-hand understanding in the face of creation in the season of *CONCEIVING SPIRIT*.

V. The Sequence Of Seasons

Advancing into new lands,
the true self imprints its presence on every moment.

After things have been sown in further lands, they are watered with the stream of attention:
CONCENTRATING ATTENTION is the focus of energy.

VI. The Souls' Journey

Ball lightning passes into the mountainside and emerges again in seven seasons:
The guardians stand watch at the four corners during the guide's pilgrimage.

VII. The Inertial Lines

Eight in the First Place:

One breaks through
when one sees through.

Savants expect the other realm to present itself.

Eight in the Second Place:

When the pack howls
the herd circles the young.

One recognizes threats to the most vulnerable ahead of time.

Seven in the Third Place:

Taken captive by the present,
addicted to the medicine.

The great-souled free themselves even from what they revere.

Seven in the Fourth Place:

The forest pathways
*   are old as the forest.*

The ways of intent help shape the world.

Eight in the Fifth Place:

The moon passes effortlessly
*   through all the phases of mind.*

The cycles of change are not apart from thought.

Eight in the Sixth Place:

The well of light
*   has no bottom.*

Dispense benefit from the inextinguishable source.

SEASON 14
UNLOCKING EVOLUTION

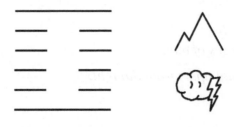

OUTER NATURE: **MOUNTAIN**
INNER NATURE: **LIGHTNING**

I. MANTIC FORMULA

Lightning within, Mountain without: The season of UNLOCKING EVOLUTION arrives. Success comes to those who are part of a wider community of visionaries.

The butterfly is born after a difficult labor: The situation is one of an inner transformation breaking an outer stalemate.

You ascend another rung of the ladder: The soul who cannot be beaten by an unbeatable foe achieves victory on an unblooded battlefield in the season of UNLOCKING EVOLUTION.

II. JUXTAPOSITION OF SEQUENCES

Toltec I Ching Hexagram #14   King Wen Hexagram #14
Unlocking Evolution   Possession in Great Measure

Upper Trigram: Mountain   Upper Trigram: Fire
Lower Trigram: Lightning   Lower Trigram: Sun

III. EVOLUTION OF SEQUENCE

Mountain stands in the place of Fire above, Lightning stands in the place of Sun below: That which is endowed with greatness unlocks the pent-up forces of metamorphosis.

IV. EVOLUTION OF HEXAGRAM

Hexagram #27 Trusting Intuition resolves the personal power of POSSESSION IN GREAT MEASURE by returning its generative energy to the spiritual senses. Sun facing Fire was power controlled by wisdom in POSSESSION IN GREAT MEASURE—but is transformed into incipient change in the face of clear-sighted perception in the season of *TRUSTING INTUITION*.

V. THE SEQUENCE OF SEASONS

Staying awake every step,
the true self is unexpectedly catapulted to the end of the path.

After things have been transfixed, they have altered the past:
UNLOCKING EVOLUTION is the growing backwards from the inevitable.

VI. THE SOULS' JOURNEY

The mountain is riddled with secret tunnels that lead in the ten directions:
Looking back from the farthest future, the guide's path is sure and straight.

VII. THE INERTIAL LINES

Seven in the First Place:

Breaking open the dam
restores the waterwheel to life.

Spiritual vitality circulates like medicine.

Eight in the Second Place:

Talon and fang
bestow life.

Fire transmutes wood into light.

Eight in the Third Place:

Companions await
on the plateau above.

The great-souled recognize one another from afar.

Eight in the Fourth Place:

Fording a river,
*   all one's possessions on one's back.*

Lacking no resources for the challenge ahead.

Eight in the Fifth Place:

When the fever breaks,
*   new medicine is called for.*

Awakening pours out true attention.

Seven in the Sixth Place:

One's body
*   becomes a cocoon.*

The soul metamorphoses in darkness.

SEASON 15
BELONGING TOGETHER

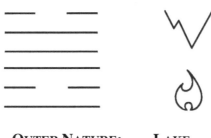

OUTER NATURE: **LAKE**
INNER NATURE: **FIRE**

I. MANTIC FORMULA

Fire within, Lake without: The season of BELONGING TOGETHER arrives. Success comes to all but those seeking separation, alienation and ill will.

Great works, both public and private, lie before you: The situation is one in which a long and difficult period of discord has ended and a new era of harmony has begun.

The umbilical road, running straight and true, stretches before you: One is blessed with the camaraderie of companions on the homebound road in the season of BELONGING TOGETHER.

II. JUXTAPOSITION OF SEQUENCES

Toltec I Ching Hexagram #15
Belonging Together

King Wen Hexagram #15
Modesty

Upper Trigram: Lake
Lower Trigram: Fire

Upper Trigram: Moon
Lower Trigram: Mountain

III. EVOLUTION OF SEQUENCE

Lake stands in the place of Moon above, Fire stands in the place of Mountain below: That which embodies true modesty is based on belonging together.

IV. Evolution of Hexagram

Hexagram #49 Staying Open resolves the just humaneness of MODESTY by returning its generative energy to open-ended development. Mountain facing Moon was sincerity amid equalizing influences in MODESTY—but is transformed into uncontrived calm in the face of open-hearted acceptance in the season of *STAYING OPEN*.

V. The Sequence Of Seasons

The lower half transmuted,
the true self rejoins the company of peers.

After things are proceeding toward their destiny, they must ensure each step is correct:
BELONGING TOGETHER is the matching of the means to the end.

VI. The Souls' Journey

The guardians carve the spirit of each stone and the traveler fits them together:
Stone by stone, from the center of the world, the two great roads are laid.

VII. The Inertial Lines

Seven in the First Place:

> *Where intimacy blooms,*
> > *butterflies and hummingbirds come to drink.*
>
> *The mind flower pollinates the world.*

Eight in the Second Place:

> *Spirit reaches,*
> > *hand touches.*
>
> *Between puppeteer and marionette, invisible strings.*

Seven in the Third Place:

> *Standing back-to-back,*
> > *allies face their own kind.*
>
> *The living and the dead occupy a single home.*

Seven in the Fourth Place:

Medicine is invisible water,
the soul nonviolent fire.

Creative imagination is the alchemical retort.

Seven in the Fifth Place:

Where order is beauty,
art, science, and religion are one.

Spirit seeks harmony with nature.

Eight in the Sixth Place:

The soul's shadow is taken captive
by the soul's light.

Ten thousand lifetimes culminate in a single laugh.

SEASON 16
RENEWING DEVOTION

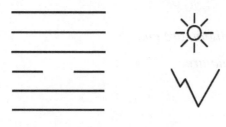

OUTER NATURE: SUN
INNER NATURE: LAKE

I. MANTIC FORMULA

Lake within, Sun without: The season of RENEWING DEVOTION arrives. Success comes to those who see through the twin mirages of fresh expectation and stale disappointment.

Do not abandon your principles: The situation is one of holding fast to the spirit of one's work.

Your loyalty to the work is the source of your strength: The medicine warrior's every act is an offering to the sacredness of everything in the season of RENEWING DEVOTION.

II. JUXTAPOSITION OF SEQUENCES

Toltec I Ching Hexagram #16
Renewing Devotion

Upper Trigram: Sun
Lower Trigram: Lake

King Wen Hexagram #16
Enthusiasm

Upper Trigram: Lightning
Lower Trigram: Moon

III. EVOLUTION OF SEQUENCE

Sun stands in the place of Lightning above, Lake stands in the place of Moon below: That which inspires sincere cooperation enjoys continually renewed devotion.

IV. Evolution of Hexagram

Hexagram #10 Unifying Inspiration resolves the social cohesion of ENTHUSIASM by returning its generative energy to creative language. Moon facing Lightning was obedience amid strong will in ENTHUSIASM—but is transformed into fulfillment in the face of incitement in the season of *UNIFYING INSPIRATION*.

V. The Sequence Of Seasons

Having gained intimacy with the collective intent,
the true self rededicates its efforts to sensing the sacredness of everything.

After things are deemed fitting, they must be pursued to the end:
RENEWING DEVOTION is the sacrificing of distractions.

VI. The Souls' Journey

A medicine warrior approaches the southern gate:
The guardians tie the city to the sun, the traveler trains to battle the enemy-within.

VII. The Inertial Lines

Seven in the First Place:

Devoted to fear—
the walls must come down.

The tiger cub is fully grown.

Seven in the Second Place:

Devoted to hope—
the walls must be raised.

An open drawbridge invites exploiters.

Eight in the Third Place:

Devoted to grief—
the way back must be closed.

The past cannot be carried into the present.

Seven in the Fourth Place:

> *Devoted to duty—*
> > *the way forward must be opened.*
>
> *The present cannot be carried into the future.*

Seven in the Fifth Place:

> *Devoted to discipline—*
> > *tears must give way to laughter.*
>
> *The ordeal opens the heart to its innate perfectibility.*

Seven in the Sixth Place:

> *Devoted to freedom—*
> > *laughter must give way to tears.*
>
> *The road of immortality passes through the gate of mortality.*

SEASON 17
GUIDING FORCE

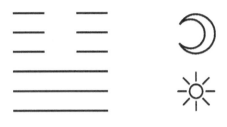

OUTER NATURE: MOON
INNER NATURE: SUN

I. MANTIC FORMULA

Sun within, Moon without: The season of GUIDING FORCE arrives. Success comes to those daring enough to initiate a new era.

Your own light guides your way: The situation is one of exploring the unknown.

You are a torch for others: Those who embody the best traits of daring and self-sacrifice have been long and painstakingly prepared for this journey through the season of GUIDING FORCE.

II. JUXTAPOSITION OF SEQUENCES

Toltec I Ching Hexagram #17
Guiding Force

Upper Trigram: Moon
Lower Trigram: Sun

King Wen Hexagram #17
Following

Upper Trigram: Lake
Lower Trigram: Lightning

III. EVOLUTION OF SEQUENCE

Moon stands in the place of Lake above, Sun stands in the place of Lightning below: That which meets with no resistance becomes a guiding force through the unknown.

IV. Evolution of Hexagram

Hexagram #11 Attracting Allies resolves the timely adaptation of FOLLOWING by returning its generative energy to sacred work. Lightning facing Lake was movement amid cooperation in FOLLOWING—but is transformed into inspiration in the face of collaboration in the season of *ATTRACTING ALLIES*.

V. The Sequence Of Seasons

Stepping into the spirit realm,
the true self trusts the dream body to lead the way.

After things have been followed consistently, they become ingrained:
GUIDING FORCE is the power to keep one's bearings in the invisible.

VI. The Souls' Journey

Sky and earth are turned upside down:
The guide finds the map of time and returns it to the traveler.

VII. The Inertial Lines

Seven in the First Place:

Daring souls
> *do not hold their allies back.*

Generosity of spirit promotes others.

Seven in the Second Place:

Daring souls
> *cannot be held back by ghosts.*

Courageous spirits carry only the present with them.

Seven in the Third Place:

Daring souls
> *do not chase victories.*

Victorious spirits have nothing to gamble.

Eight in the Fourth Place:

Daring souls
do not walk in their own tracks.

Penetrating spirits find no old moments.

Eight in the Fifth Place:

Daring souls
are the vanguard.

Headlong spirits arrive in a single step.

Eight in the Sixth Place:

Daring souls
return unscathed but not untouched.

Medicine spirits do not flinch from wounds.

SEASON 18
RESOLVING PARADOX

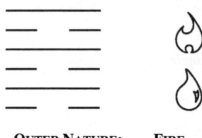

OUTER NATURE: FIRE
INNER NATURE: WATER

I. MANTIC FORMULA

Water within, Fire without: The season of RESOLVING PARADOX arrives. Success comes to those who act on the knowledge that the world is alive and aware.

Pursue the way of coincidences: The situation is one of rediscovering the fate of freedom.

Plumb your dreams: The medicine warrior, fated to awaken between lives, emulates the creative nature of the first ancestors in the season of RESOLVING PARADOX.

II. JUXTAPOSITION OF SEQUENCES

Toltec I Ching Hexagram #18
Resolving Paradox

Upper Trigram: Fire
Lower Trigram: Water

King Wen Hexagram #18
Work on What Has Been Spoiled [Decay]

Upper Trigram: Mountain
Lower Trigram: Wind

III. EVOLUTION OF SEQUENCE

Fire stands in the place of Mountain above, Water stands in the place of Wind below: That which sincerely strives to right old wrongs resolves the paradox of mutually-exclusive polarities.

IV. EVOLUTION OF HEXAGRAM

Hexagram #64 Safeguarding Life resolves the determined reform of WORK ON WHAT HAS BEEN SPOILED by returning its generative energy to universal reverence. Wind facing Mountain was persuasion amid consolidation in WORK ON WHAT HAS BEEN SPOILED—but is transformed into ongoing adaptation in the face of ongoing resistance in the season of *SAFEGUARDING LIFE*.

V. THE SEQUENCE OF SEASONS

Passing whole through the unknown,
the true self merges with the great mystery.

After things have been ordered in the invisible, they irrupt as accidents in the visible:
RESOLVING PARADOX is the attunement of the senses to the irrational.

VI. THE SOULS' JOURNEY

A moat of burning water:
The enemy-within is a shape-shifter.

VII. THE INERTIAL LINES

Eight in the First Place:

The inability to accept paradox
is a hallmark of the troubled spirit.

The desire for certainty is the cornerstone of ignorance.

Seven in the Second Place:

Once a horse's spirit is broken,
it will never race again.

Savants train the passions without taming them.

Eight in the Third Place:

One contains
one's own contradiction.

It leapfrogs over itself.

Seven in the Fourth Place:

> *One's lifework depends*
> > *on one's creative use of distractions.*
>
> *Everything is part of the same river rushing to the same sea.*

Eight in the Fifth Place:

> *Tyranny springs ever anew*
> > *from materialism.*
>
> *One aligns with the inevitable turning point.*

Seven in the Sixth Place:

> *The work is a riddle*
> > *whose answer is the work.*
>
> *The inner master alone knows the way.*

SEASON 19
CELEBRATING PASSAGE

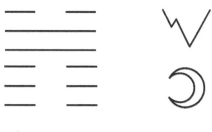

OUTER NATURE: **LAKE**
INNER NATURE: **MOON**

I. MANTIC FORMULA

Moon within, Lake without: The season of CELEBRATING PASSAGE arrives. Success comes to those who drink from the well of joy.

Your heart comes to full bloom: The situation is one of cultivating a spirit that conscientiously recognizes and honors the landmarks of one's lifetime.

Embody the jaguar by night and the eagle by day: The soul forces time itself to pause in order to consecrate the past and dedicate the future during the season of CELEBRATING PASSAGE.

II. JUXTAPOSITION OF SEQUENCES

Toltec I Ching Hexagram #19
Celebrating Passage

King Wen Hexagram #19
Approach

Upper Trigram: Lake
Lower Trigram: Moon

Upper Trigram: Moon
Lower Trigram: Lake

III. EVOLUTION OF SEQUENCE

Lake stands in the place of Moon above, Moon stands in the place of Lake below: That which gains ascendancy maintains humaneness by celebrating the cyclic passages of body and spirit.

IV. Evolution of Hexagram

Hexagram #45 Casting Off resolves the growing progress of APPROACH by returning its generative energy to joyous completion. Lake facing Moon was joyous amid devotion in APPROACH—but is transformed into wonder in the face of completion in the season of *CASTING OFF*.

V. The Sequence Of Seasons

At one with the timeless,
the true self rejoices in the cycles of time.

After things are cut loose from the anchor of reason, they face an unbroken horizon of joy:
CELEBRATING PASSAGE is the rejoicing in rites of passage.

VI. The Souls' Journey

The traveler survives the ordeal of water:
The medicine warrior bestows a jade shield.

VII. The Inertial Lines

Eight in the First Place:

Those without guile
are destined for greatness.

Those already content are without ulterior motive.

Eight in the Second Place:

Communities are bound together
by sanctioned revelry.

The dance recounts every dancer.

Eight in the Third Place:

The annual recurrence of shared rituals
grounds the community in cyclic time.

The superficial runs deep.

Seven in the Fourth Place:

Uninterrupted revelry
breeds its opposite.

True freedom does not enslave the senses.

Seven in the Fifth Place:

Sacred rituals
unite the visible and the invisible.

Souls ascend, spirits descend, along the world axis.

Eight in the Sixth Place:

When ritual becomes empty form,
the sacred seeks out a new vessel.

An open heart remains the lodging-place for the sacred.

SEASON 20
ENTERING SERVICE

OUTER NATURE: **WATER**
INNER NATURE: **LAKE**

I. MANTIC FORMULA

Lake within, Water without: The season of ENTERING SERVICE arrives. Success comes to those who materially assist others in obtaining what they most need.

You undertake a new endeavor: The situation is one of hardship and want that were anticipated beforehand.

Build for others: Great and noble works will be the legacy of those who daily perform simple acts of sincere compassion in the season of ENTERING SERVICE.

II. JUXTAPOSITION OF SEQUENCES

Toltec I Ching Hexagram #20
Entering Service

King Wen Hexagram #20
Contemplation [View]

Upper Trigram: Water
Lower Trigram: Lake

Upper Trigram: Wind
Lower Trigram: Moon

III. EVOLUTION OF SEQUENCE

Water stands in the place of Wind above, Lake stands in the place of Moon below: That which is worthy of contemplation finds itself entering service.

IV. Evolution of Hexagram

Hexagram #60 Changing Alliances resolves the charismatic leadership of CONTEMPLATION by returning its generative energy to withdrawing allegiance. Moon facing Wind was compliance amid influence in CONTEMPLATION—but is transformed into completing a cycle in the face of evolving adaptation in the season of *CHANGING ALLIANCES*.

V. The Sequence Of Seasons

At one with the joys and sorrows of life,
the true self returns wholeheartedly to serving the best interests of all.

After things have been treasured for their timelessness, they set sail again on the tides of time:
ENTERING SERVICE is the ordaining of a new mandate.

VI. The Souls' Journey

The traveler and the guide are reunited:
The medicine warrior vows fealty to the guardians and the founding ritual is performed.

VII. The Inertial Lines

Seven in the First Place:

Beginnings are wasted on those
who use them to get their bearings.

The first glimpse never occurs twice.

Seven in the Second Place:

Guiding principles
must inspire a change of heart.

Real practice is transformative.

Eight in the Third Place:

Foreboding, when properly amplified,
is transformed into awe.

Everyone is always facing the infinity of outer space.

Eight in the Fourth Place:

> *The old gives way to the new*
> *and the compass points change places.*

> *The moment before reorientation should be prolonged.*

Seven in the Fifth Place:

> *New protocols must be established*
> *before the vision fades.*

> *Ethics born of insight benefit all.*

Eight in the Sixth Place:

> *The beginning itself is the secret,*
> *the planting of seeds is the work.*

> *Sowing the field of intention inevitably yields fruit.*

SEASON 21
CULTIVATING CHARACTER

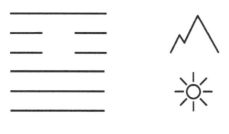

OUTER NATURE: **MOUNTAIN**
INNER NATURE: **SUN**

I. MANTIC FORMULA

Sun within, Mountain without: The season of CULTIVATING CHARACTER arrives. Success comes to those who conscientiously undertake the further refinement of their nature.

Advance within: The situation is one in which opportunity for external progress is postponed.

Circulate the currents of hot and cold within you: The invisible pathways between the realms of nature, human nature, and the supernatural become tangible in the season of CULTIVATING CHARACTER.

II. JUXTAPOSITION OF SEQUENCES

Toltec I Ching Hexagram #21
Cultivating Character

King Wen Hexagram #21
Biting Through

Upper Trigram: Mountain
Lower Trigram: Sun

Upper Trigram: Fire
Lower Trigram: Lightning

III. EVOLUTION OF SEQUENCE

Mountain stands in the place of Fire above, Sun stands in the place of Lightning below: That which enforces codes of conduct passes through the crucible of cultivating character.

IV. Evolution of Hexagram

Hexagram #26 Dignifying Ambition resolves the punished wrong-doing of BITING THROUGH by returning its generative energy to ennobling longings. Lightning facing Fire was movement amid beliefs in BITING THROUGH—but is transformed into pure intent in the face of wisdom in the season of *DIGNIFYING AMBITION.*

V. The Sequence Of Seasons

In order to bring the best to others,
the true self works steadfastly to purify its perception and intent.

After things have accepted their calling, they prepare for the unforeseen storm:
CULTIVATING CHARACTER is the perfection of the spirit of readiness.

VI. The Souls' Journey

A midwife appears at the western gate, accompanied by the spider and the serpent:
The fields are tilled but there is no seed for planting.

VII. The Inertial Lines

Seven in the First Place:

Utterly relaxed, the coiled serpent
is nonetheless poised to strike.

The still point is the pivot between nonaction and action.

Seven in the Second Place:

One cannot imagine
what one is being readied for.

The wise are attuned to the gravitational pull of the future.

Seven in the Third Place:

Being unprepared is a sign of rashness,
being over-prepared is a sign of fear.

The self-sufficient improvise with what they have.

Eight in the Fourth Place:

What is not instinctual
    is superstitious.

The mystic attunes to perception, not conception.

Eight in the Fifth Place:

Spirit overflows its body
    like water overflowing a well.

The hermit crab moves from a smaller shell to a larger shell.

Seven in the Sixth Place:

Any culture that believes itself civilized
    is barbaric.

The powerful are impaired by their drunkenness.

SEASON 22
SHARING MEMORY

OUTER NATURE: **FIRE**
INNER NATURE: **MOUNTAIN**

I. MANTIC FORMULA

Mountain within, Fire without: The season of SHARING MEMORY arrives. Success comes to those who sit in council when alone.

Your voice is part of the choir: The situation is one in which the present awakens to the meeting place of spirits.

Unearth the buried treasure: Those with a tranquil mind and untroubled heart are able to tap the living reservoir of radiant awareness in the season of SHARING MEMORY.

II. JUXTAPOSITION OF SEQUENCES

Toltec I Ching Hexagram #22
Sharing Memory

Upper Trigram: Fire
Lower Trigram: Mountain

King Wen Hexagram #22
Grace

Upper Trigram: Mountain
Lower Trigram: Fire

III. EVOLUTION OF SEQUENCE

Fire stands in the place of Mountain above, Mountain stands in the place of Fire below: That which adorns the essential emerges from ancestral memory.

74

IV. Evolution of Hexagram

Hexagram #56 Recapturing Vision resolves the relative merit of GRACE by returning its generative energy to reawakened idealism. Fire facing Mountain was fleeting light amid stable density in GRACE—but is transformed into insight in the face of tranquility in the season of *RECAPTURING VISION*.

V. The Sequence Of Seasons

Emptied of outworn perceptions and intentions,
the true self becomes a receptacle for the shared memories of creation.

After things are given ballast, they navigate without star or compass:
SHARING MEMORY is the discovery of veiled experiences.

VI. The Souls' Journey

Smoke rises from the sacred mountain:
The temple is erected and offerings burnt.

VII. The Inertial Lines

Eight in the First Place:

One is remembered forever
for what one dedicated one's life to.

One's true purpose shines like a signal fire on the hill.

Eight in the Second Place:

Remembering less and less of one's life
allows older memories to enter.

The ancients do not forget the living.

Seven in the Third Place:

Spaces of time without a single memory
are a hallmark of the untroubled spirit.

Peace of mind leaps from one moment to the next.

Seven in the Fourth Place:

Memories
*   have a mind of their own.*

Collective experience builds its own cathedral.

Eight in the Fifth Place:

History is the seedbed
*   of artificial identity.*

The true self must remember itself.

Seven in the Sixth Place:

The art of remembering lies
*   in the dream body's mobility.*

Pure awareness does not identify with a single memory.

SEASON 23
WIELDING PASSION

OUTER NATURE: FIRE
INNER NATURE: LAKE

I. MANTIC FORMULA

Lake within, Fire without: The season of WIELDING PASSION arrives. Success comes to those who are able to be content without sacrificing their longings.

Do not neglect your need to desire: The situation is one in which goals are achieved—and can be sustained indefinitely—through the consistent execution of surprise actions.

What does not burn, dies out: Great disasters may be avoided by those who value the life-affirming forces driving human nature in the season of WIELDING PASSION.

II. JUXTAPOSITION OF SEQUENCES

Toltec I Ching Hexagram #23
Wielding Passion

Upper Trigram: Fire
Lower Trigram: Lake

King Wen Hexagram #23
Splitting Apart

Upper Trigram: Mountain
Lower Trigram: Moon

III. EVOLUTION OF SEQUENCE

Fire stands in the place of Mountain above, Lake stands in the place of Moon below: That which displaces the obsolete opens the way to new adventures.

IV. EVOLUTION OF HEXAGRAM

Hexagram #38 Dissolving Artifice resolves the disintegrating influence of SPLITTING APART by returning its generative energy to discovering identity. Moon facing Mountain was passiveness amid disruption in SPLITTING APART—but is transformed into completion of a cycle in the face of calm contemplation in the season of *DISSOLVING ARTIFICE*.

V. THE SEQUENCE OF SEASONS

Steeped in the realm of past lives,
the true self fathoms the primacy of the creative longings.

After things have been fully explored, they reach the limits of meaning:
WIELDING PASSION is the borderland between the known and the unknown.

VI. THE SOULS' JOURNEY

A meteor falls into the city:
The midwife bathes it in the spider web and swaddles it in the whirlwind.

VII. THE INERTIAL LINES

Seven in the First Place:

Nothing is so irrational
that it cannot be rationalized away.

Civilization is built on the ruins of nobler dreams.

Seven in the Second Place:

One's greatest weakness, when properly amplified,
is one's greatest strength.

The clearest water lies at the bottom of the well.

Eight in the Third Place:

One cannot control events
but one can control one's reactions to them.

The ecstatic life arises from calm equilibrium.

Seven in the Fourth Place:

All but the weakest lemmings
rush toward the precipice.

Competition inevitably proves self-destructive.

Eight in the Fifth Place:

Symbols are the footprints
of spirit.

Form itself is symbol.

Seven in the Sixth Place:

Idealizing the future
is an attempt to keep it at arm's length.

The pyramid is built one stone at a time.

SEASON 24
REVEALING KNOWLEDGE

OUTER NATURE: **LAKE**
INNER NATURE: **SUN**

I. MANTIC FORMULA

Sun within, Lake without: The season of REVEALING KNOWLEDGE arrives. Success comes to those who come face-to-face with the hidden.

Your vision benefits all: The situation is one in which the future gives up its secrets to the present.

Build your dwelling upon the moment of epiphany: The sacred unmasks itself in the season of REVEALING KNOWLEDGE.

II. JUXTAPOSITION OF SEQUENCES

Toltec I Ching Hexagram #24
Revealing Knowledge

King Wen Hexagram #24
Return [The Turning Point]

Upper Trigram: Lake
Lower Trigram: Sun

Upper Trigram: Moon
Lower Trigram: Lightning

III. EVOLUTION OF SEQUENCE

Lake stands in the place of Moon above, Sun stands in the place of Lightning below: That which returns, reveals.

80

IV. Evolution of Hexagram

Hexagram #43 Going Beyond resolves the cyclic arrival of Return by returning its generative energy to unceasing transcendence. Lightning facing Moon was movement with devotion in Return—but is transformed into forceful motivation in the face of cyclic completion in the season of *Going Beyond*.

V. The Sequence Of Seasons

The passion for creative union leads the true self
to witness the single act of creation.

After things have reached their extremes, they encounter the ancient novelty:
Revealing Knowledge is the return to the primordial act of creation.

VI. The Souls' Journey

The sun passes into the underworld through the sacred cave:
The serpent sheds its skin and rises, to become the morning star.

VII. The Inertial Lines

Seven in the First Place:

If it cannot be approached by everyone,
then it is not the truth.

Innate illumination is the universal birthright.

Seven in the Second Place:

An instant of illumination
dispels the darkness of a lifetime.

A lightning flash irrevocably transforms the night landscape.

Seven in the Third Place:

The primordial act of creation
is the present moment.

It is all a continuous eternal surging.

Seven in the Fourth Place:

Neither the vision nor its reflection that must be polished,
*   but the mirror.*

Pure awareness embodies space.

Seven in the Fifth Place:

One orbits
*   the sacred.*

The open secret eludes words.

Eight in the Sixth Place:

The frog cannot see what does not move,
*   the mind cannot perceive what does not change.*

The heartbeat of the song of the universe never wavers.

SEASON 25
RADIATING INTENT

OUTER NATURE: LIGHTNING
INNER NATURE: SUN

I. MANTIC FORMULA

Sun within, Lightning without: The season of RADIATING INTENT arrives. Success comes to all.

Your heart is the sun's target: The situation is one of enlightened cooperation, collaboration, and compassion.

Approach every ordeal the way the jaguar approaches the rabbit: The sacred uninterruptedly fans the flame of all living beings during the season of RADIATING INTENT.

II. JUXTAPOSITION OF SEQUENCES

Toltec I Ching Hexagram #25
Radiating Intent

King Wen Hexagram #25
Innocence [The Unexpected]

Upper Trigram: Lightning
Lower Trigram: Sun

Upper Trigram: Sun
Lower Trigram: Lightning

III. EVOLUTION OF SEQUENCE

Lightning stands in the place of Sun above, Sun stands in the place of Lightning below: That which strives to transcend striving radiates magnanimous intent.

IV. EVOLUTION OF HEXAGRAM

Hexagram #34 Evoking Opposite resolves the uncontrived virtue of INNOCENCE by returning its generative energy to spiritual protection. Lightning facing the Sun was unforeseen movement amid purposeful strength in INNOCENCE—but is transformed into motivating action in the face of spiritual potential in the season of *EVOKING OPPOSITE*.

V. THE SEQUENCE OF SEASONS

The mystic lightning bolt illuminates the true self
as an idea reverberating throughout eternity.

After things have been charged with the ancient intent, they beckon through the fog and night:
RADIATING INTENT is the lighthouse on the shore of one's homeland.

VI. THE SOULS' JOURNEY

Lightning falls from the morning star and strikes its own twin:
The serpent's shed skin rises, to become the evening star.

VII. THE INERTIAL LINES

Seven in the First Place:

> *The world soul lives thoroughly immersed*
> *in the sacred.*

> *Dreaming psyche has not yet bifurcated into waking and sleeping.*

Seven in the Second Place:

> *The world soul lives closer to the time creation,*
> *it is a newer realm.*

> *Dreaming psyche steps back into the sphere of the creators.*

Seven in the Third Place:

> *The descendants live further from the time of creation,*
> *in an older realm.*

> *The first voices give way to their echoes.*

84

Seven in the Fourth Place:

The world soul lies beyond an ancient road,
        at the center of the maze.

The inner compass points to the mystical.

Eight in the Fifth Place:

The world soul is roused in time
        to gather the descendants back to the origin.

Universal change of heart cannot be postponed indefinitely.

Eight in the Sixth Place:

The descendants live thoroughly immersed
        in the sacred.

As within, so without.

SEASON 26
DIGNIFYING AMBITION

OUTER NATURE: FIRE
INNER NATURE: LIGHTNING

I. MANTIC FORMULAS

Lightning within, Fire without: The season of DIGNIFYING AMBITION arrives. Success comes to those able to walk away from it at every turn.

Your vehicle must match your goal: The situation is one in which worthy endeavors ensure personal advancement.

The highest ambitions attract the most powerful adversaries: One's character is fully revealed in the season of DIGNIFYING AMBITION.

II. JUXTAPOSITION OF SEQUENCES

Toltec I Ching Hexagram #26
Dignifying Ambition

King Wen Hexagram #26
The Taming Power of the Great

Upper Trigram: Fire
Lower Trigram: Lightning

Upper Trigram: Mountain
Lower Trigram: Sun

III. EVOLUTION OF SEQUENCE

Fire stands in the place of Mountain above, Lightning stands in the place of Sun below: That which accumulates resources must ennoble ambition.

IV. EVOLUTION OF HEXAGRAM

Hexagram #21 Cultivating Character resolves the growing energy of THE TAMING POWER OF THE GREAT by returning its generative energy to perfecting intent. Sun facing Mountain was great strength being held firm in THE TAMING POWER OF THE GREAT—but is transformed into creative potential in the face of stable tranquility in the season of *CULTIVATING CHARACTER*.

V. THE SEQUENCE OF SEASONS

Casting out into the field of intent,
the true self ensures the nobility of its intent.

After things have traced their lineage, they wish to contribute to its posterity:
DIGNIFYING AMBITION is the desire to pass on the inheritance.

VI. THE SOULS' JOURNEY

The traveler survives the ordeal by fire:
The medicine warrior bestows a necklace of jade beads.

VII. THE INERTIAL LINES

Seven in the First Place:

They lead because they follow
a superior morality.

Even the fates are moved to change course.

Eight in the Second Place:

They lose ground because they fall back
on long-standing resentments.

Self-righteousness is self-defeating.

Eight in the Third Place:

They are attacked because they threaten
others' beliefs.

Ignorance is easily mistaken for arrogance.

Seven in the Fourth Place:

> *They are followed because they offer*
> > *the only alternative to stagnation.*
>
> *Change and change for the better are not the same thing.*

Eight in the Fifth Place:

> *They govern because they are dedicated*
> > *to the equality of all things.*
>
> *The inevitable good always accords with the underlying harmony.*

Seven in the Sixth Place:

> *They are attacked because they threaten*
> > *the foundation of the palace.*
>
> *Disinterestedness is easily mistaken for antipathy.*

SEASON 27
TRUSTING INTUITION

OUTER NATURE:	**FIRE**
INNER NATURE:	**SUN**

I. MANTIC FORMULA

Sun within, Fire without: The season of TRUSTING INTUITION arrives. Success comes to those already dwelling in the future.

Avoid the present: The situation is one of conflicting premonitions regarding impending events.

Your sincerity is your shield: The future haunts the present in the season of TRUSTING INTUITION.

II. JUXTAPOSITION OF SEQUENCES

Toltec I Ching Hexagram #27
Trusting Intuition

King Wen Hexagram #27
Corners of the Mouth [Providing Nourishment]

Upper Trigram: Fire
Lower Trigram: Sun

Upper Trigram: Mountain
Lower Trigram: Lightning

III. EVOLUTION OF SEQUENCE

Fire stands in the place of Mountain above, Sun stands in the place of Lightning below: That which seeks to nurture the best succeeds only by trusting the deeper senses.

IV. Evolution of Hexagram

Hexagram #14 Unlocking Evolution resolves the nurturing attention of Corners of the Mouth by returning its generative energy to the metamorphic breakthrough. Lightning facing Mountain was forceful movement against firm resistance in Corners of the Mouth—but is transformed into inspiration in the face of incubation in the season of *Unlocking Evolution*.

V. The Sequence of Seasons

In accord with the one intent,
the true self responds to each moment by feel.

After things are sought for the benefit of the future, they cannot be found with the five senses:
Trusting Intuition is the capacity to track the footprints of the invisible.

VI. The Souls' Journey

The evening star leads the sun on its journey through the underworld:
The traveler receives from the sun the secret of its sacred fire.

VII. The Inertial Lines

Seven in the First Place:

Impressions take root
> *outside.*

Lightning leaves its fingerprints in fused sand.

Seven in the Second Place:

Prophecies are fueled
> *by hope and fear.*

True diviners eschew personal feelings.

Seven in the Third Place:

Cultural changes come in response
> *to predictable crises.*

Few see the foresigns of incipiency.

Seven in the Fourth Place:

Self-governance begins when the individual
moves toward the inevitable future.

The human soul and the world soul reunite.

Eight in the Fifth Place:

The future is entrusted to those
who can envision its beauty.

The past is a superstition.

Seven in the Sixth Place:

It is the constant pull toward resignation
that charges the spirit to fly.

In the end, doubt doubts doubt.

SEASON 28
SYNCHRONIZING MOVEMENT

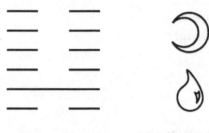

OUTER NATURE:	**MOON**
INNER NATURE:	**WATER**

I. MANTIC FORMULA

Water within, Moon without: The season of SYNCHRONIZING MOVEMENT arrives. Success comes to those who overcome their suspicion of others' motives.

Pull together on the yoke: The situation is one in which greater harmony is achieved through an alignment of common interests.

Keep time to the heartbeat of the sacred: The simultaneity of things dispels the illusion of their incompatibility in the season of SYNCHRONIZING MOVEMENT.

II. JUXTAPOSITION OF SEQUENCES

Toltec I Ching Hexagram #28
Synchronizing Movement

King Wen Hexagram #28
Preponderance of the Great

Upper Trigram: Moon
Lower Trigram: Water

Upper Trigram: Lake
Lower Trigram: Wind

III. EVOLUTION OF SEQUENCE

Moon stands in the place of Lake above, Water stands in the place of Wind below: That which strains beneath its own weight must align with the underlying rhythm of change.

IV. Evolution of Hexagram

Hexagram #7 Compelling Motive resolves the excessive strain of Preponderance of the Great by returning its generative energy to welcoming change. Wind facing Lake was aloneness while undaunted in Preponderance of the Great—but is transformed into adaptation in the face of passion in the season of *Compelling Motive*.

V. The Sequence of Seasons

Acting without premeditation or contrivance,
the true self changes with the rhythm of change.

After things have pierced the veil of time, they return to the rhythm of space:
Synchronizing Movement is the attunement of the senses to the unchanging.

VI. The Souls' Journey

The morning star leads the sun out of the underworld into a new dawn:
The traveler returns from the shadow realm with colored seeds for planting time.

VII. The Inertial Lines

Eight in the First Place:

One caretakes the dwelling-place
and waits for the host.

Stewards of change build a nest for the phoenix.

Seven in the Second Place:

One keeps time
with the spirit of nature.

The grand cycle of eternity turns with every breath.

Eight in the Third Place:

Rising out of the choir,
the solo voice sails.

Collective genius gives birth to individual genius.

93

Eight in the Fourth Place:

The whetstone of propriety
dulls the blade of truth.

Truth should scratch the eardrums.

Eight in the Fifth Place:

Things that do not belong together
should not necessarily be broken apart.

Things that happen at the same time have a secret alliance.

Eight in the Sixth Place:

One works
in invisible partnership.

The holy guardian messenger pulls back the veil.

SEASON 29
SUSTAINING RESILIENCE

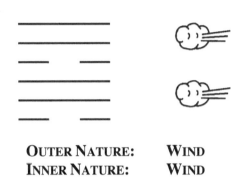

OUTER NATURE: WIND
INNER NATURE: WIND

I. MANTIC FORMULA

Wind within, Wind without: The season of SUSTAINING RESILIENCE arrives. Success comes to all who adapt to obstacles with the fluidly of the wind.

Your curiosity guides you: The situation is one of discovery leading out of hardship.

Mimic the plants of the wild: The medicine warrior likens fate's whims to a parent's loving-kindness in the season of SUSTAINING RESILIENCE.

II. JUXTAPOSITION OF SEQUENCES

Toltec I Ching Hexagram #29
Sustaining Resilience

Upper Trigram: Wind
Lower Trigram: Wind

King Wen Hexagram #29
The Abysmal [Water]

Upper Trigram: Water
Lower Trigram: Water

III. EVOLUTION OF SEQUENCE

Wind stands in the place of Water above, Wind stands in the place of Water below: That which survives danger perfects adaptability.

IV. Evolution of Hexagram

Hexagram #57 Defying Uncertainty resolves the harrowing passage of THE ABYSMAL by returning its generative energy to the untroubled spirit. Water facing Water was danger upon danger in THE ABYSMAL—but is transformed into unfathomable mystery in the face of unfathomable mystery in the season of *DEFYING UNCERTAINTY*.

V. The Sequence of Seasons

In harmony with the current of creation,
the true self adapts to prolonged trials with utmost flexibility.

After things proceed together, their expansion cannot be confined:
SUSTAINING RESILIENCE is the power to assume any form.

VI. The Souls' Journey

The seeds are sown and harvested in the same day:
Each yields a different fruit that transforms the traveler's dream body.

VII. The Inertial Lines

Eight in the First Place:

Without a fixed identity, the eye is a mirror
reflecting only whatever is before it.

The looking glass holds no past reflections.

Seven in the Second Place:

Good fortune benefits only those
who give it away without hesitation.

Misfortune follows hoarders of good fortune.

Seven in the Third Place:

Wind and water
flow without intent.

Pure intent adapts itself to changing circumstances.

96

Eight in the Fourth Place:

> *Enough nuggets*
> *   fashion a mountain.*
>
> *Great deeds arise from accumulated surprises.*

Seven in the Fifth Place:

> *Flexible without, unswerving within—*
> *   perfect purpose.*
>
> *One with change is a majority.*

Seven in the Sixth Place:

> *Spirit knows*
> *   no bounds.*
>
> *One is a mystery unto oneself.*

SEASON 30
TRANSFORMING EXTINCTION

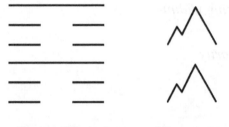

OUTER NATURE:	**MOUNTAIN**
INNER NATURE:	**MOUNTAIN**

I. MANTIC FORMULA

Mountain within, Mountain without: The season of TRANSFORMING EXTINCTION arrives. Success comes to those who see through endings.

Ascend the sacred mountain: The situation is one of integrating death, destruction, and dissolution into a higher order.

Mimic the cocoon: The life of the caterpillar comes to an end in the season of TRANSFORMING EXTINCTION.

II. JUXTAPOSITION OF SEQUENCES

Toltec I Ching Hexagram #30	King Wen Hexagram #30
Transforming Extinction	The Clinging, Fire

Upper Trigram: Mountain	Upper Trigram: Fire
Lower Trigram: Mountain	Lower Trigram: Fire

III. EVOLUTION OF SEQUENCE

Mountain stands in the place of Fire above, Mountain stands in the place of Fire below: That which burns brightest transforms the shadow.

IV. Evolution of Hexagram

Hexagram #52 Growing Certainty resolves the voluntary dependence of THE CLINGING by returning its generative energy to evolving understandings. Fire facing Fire was fragile brightness upon fragile brightness in THE CLINGING—but is transformed into individual truth in the face of universal truth in the season of *GROWING CERTAINTY*.

V. THE SEQUENCE OF SEASONS

Surviving every ordeal,
the true self embodies the spirit of metamorphosis.

After things have expanded to the utmost, their contraction cannot be confined:
TRANSFORMING EXTINCTION is the power to assume no form.

VI. THE SOULS' JOURNEY

A single seed is planted beneath the temple:
Its vine produces a bitter fruit that transforms the dream body into the dreamer.

VII. THE INERTIAL LINES

Eight in the First Place:

Though the sun rises,
the stars still course the night.

The dream body accompanies the waking self.

Eight in the Second Place:

Traits necessary for survival must be discarded
once they have outlived their purpose.

The world's loving-kindness embodies the world soul's.

Seven in the Third Place:

Spirit, time and number
are one.

Every day is a divine presence.

Eight in the Fourth Place:

Dreams
            are a parallel life.

Creative imagination unites the two lives.

Eight in the Fifth Place:

The panacea
            transforms poison into medicine.

The philosopher's stone transmutes self-interest into empathy.

Seven in the Sixth Place:

The spirit of nature
            ever circulates.

It rests by changing.

SEASON 31
EMBRACING NONINTERFERENCE

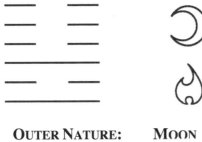

OUTER NATURE:	**MOON**
INNER NATURE:	**FIRE**

I. MANTIC FORMULA

Fire within, Moon without: The season of EMBRACING NONINTERFERENCE arrives. Success comes to all but those who are threatened by the success of others.

You emulate the great mother: The situation is one in which people are allowed to develop naturally without any interference from others.

You balance freedom and responsibility: The work of perfecting the community of spirit is renewed in the season of EMBRACING NONINTERFERENCE.

II. JUXTAPOSITION OF SEQUENCES

Toltec I Ching Hexagram #31
Embracing Noninterference

Upper Trigram: Moon
Lower Trigram: Fire

King Wen Hexagram #31
Influence [Wooing]

Upper Trigram: Lake
Lower Trigram: Mountain

III. EVOLUTION OF SEQUENCE

Moon stands in the place of Lake above, Fire stands in the place of Mountain below: That which is most far-reaching brings unconditional benefit.

IV. Evolution of Hexagram

Hexagram #36 Stabilizing Communion resolves the reciprocal attraction of INFLUENCE by returning its generative energy to lasting at-one-ment. Mountain facing Lake was stability amid enthusiasm in INFLUENCE—but is transformed into tranquil contemplation in the face of grateful appreciation in the season of *STABILIZING COMMUNION*.

V. The Sequence of Seasons

Identifying with metamorphosis,
the true self implements positive change without directing its effects.

After things have moved beyond confinement, they do not deny their virtue:
EMBRACING NONINTERFERENCE is the practice of compassionate neutrality.

VI. The Souls' Journey

The moon dances among the ancestor's campfires in the night sky:
The traveler keeps time with conch and rattle, compass and calendar.

VII. The Inertial Lines

Seven in the First Place:

The spirit of nature favors nothing
but diversification.

Every possibility must be explored.

Eight in the Second Place:

Good leaders establish elegant relationships
at every level.

Mutual benefit excites harmonious coordination.

Seven in the Third Place:

Failure to honor another's destiny
is an act of self-betrayal.

The alchemist separates to unite.

Eight in the Fourth Place:

The spirit of nature
is the great teacher.

The door to the treasury of symbols opens wide.

Eight in the Fifth Place:

The heart-mind of a good leader
is a lotus growing out of mud.

Selfsameness with the multitude is the law of true rule.

Eight in the Sixth Place:

Failure to judge one's own judgments
is an act of self-betrayal.

Opinions are quicksand.

SEASON 32
CONTROLLING CONFRONTATION

OUTER NATURE: SUN
INNER NATURE: WATER

I. MANTIC FORMULA

Water within, Sun without: The season of CONTROLLING CONFRONTATION arrives. Success comes to those who neither attack nor defend.

You emulate the great father: The situation is one in which people challenged by discord and strife do not reply in kind.

Move the field of battle inward: The soul transforms doubt and conflict into flawless acts of courage and compassion during the season of CONTROLLING CONFRONTATION.

II. JUXTAPOSITION OF SEQUENCES

Toltec I Ching Hexagram #32
Controlling Confrontation

King Wen Hexagram #32
Duration

Upper Trigram: Sun
Lower Trigram: Water

Upper Trigram: Lightning
Lower Trigram: Wind

III. EVOLUTION OF SEQUENCE

Sun stands in the place of Lightning above, Water stands in the place of Wind below: That which endures longest resolves conflict.

IV. Evolution of Hexagram

Hexagram #6 Fostering Self-Sacrifice resolves the recurring coupling of DURATION by returning its generative energy to sacrificing self-interest. Wind facing Lightning was devoted nonresistance amid forceful movement in DURATION—but is transformed into conscientious adaptation in the face of unexpected impetus in the season of *FOSTERING SELF-SACRIFICE*.

V. The Sequence of Seasons

Identifying with openhandedness,
the true self avoids the appearance of weakness.

After things have been accepted for their part in the whole, they reveal their true nature:
CONTROLLING CONFRONTATION is the practice of resisting force.

VI. The Souls' Journey

The sun attacks the city, causing drought and famine:
A rainmaker appears at the northern gate to do battle with the sun.

VII. The Inertial Lines

Eight in the First Place:

When people do not honor their pact with the sacred,
they turn against themselves like savages.

The universal civilizing spirit reveres all life.

Seven in the Second Place:

Justice moves
beyond precedents.

The spirit of the law does not perpetuate inequality.

Eight in the Third Place:

Never are values so clearly revealed
than when allies become enemies.

Great turning points unveil commonality.

Seven in the Fourth Place:

The powerful become clumsy and heavy-handed,
*   the powerless become deft and mercurial.*

The plodding dinosaurs give way to the flitting birds.

Seven in the Fifth Place:

Propaganda is effective only
*   when the mind is untrained.*

Savants neither believe nor disbelieve.

Seven in the Sixth Place:

Those who become accustomed to conflict
*   believe they attack others out of self-defense.*

Security is established through trust, not force.

SEASON 33
ACCEPTING INSTRUCTION

OUTER NATURE: **LIGHTNING**
INNER NATURE: **FIRE**

I. MANTIC FORMULA

Fire within, Lightning without: The season of ACCEPTING INSTRUCTION arrives. Success comes to those who choose a higher teaching.

You are what you think: The situation is one of rectifying previously learned knowledge.

Fan the flame of the new fire: The medicine warrior extinguishes every ember of the old fire before striking the first spark of the new fire during the season of ACCEPTING INSTRUCTION.

II. JUXTAPOSITION OF SEQUENCES

Toltec I Ching Hexagram #33
Accepting Instruction

Upper Trigram: Lightning
Lower Trigram: Fire

King Wen Hexagram #33
Retreat

Upper Trigram: Sun
Lower Trigram: Mountain

III. EVOLUTION OF SEQUENCE

Lightning stands in the place of Sun above, Fire stands in the place of Mountain below: That which withdraws from darkness advances into light.

IV. Evolution of Hexagram

Hexagram #55 Internalizing Purity resolves the strategic withdrawal of RETREAT by returning its generative energy to the embodied lifeway. Mountain facing Sun was intrusion amid inaccessibility in RETREAT—but is transformed into tranquil contemplation in the face of creative potential in the season of *INTERNALIZING PURITY*.

V. The Sequence of Seasons

*Seeking a way to forestall competition,
the true self studies the way of surprise.*

*After things have struggled for power, they must contend with their powerlessness:
ACCEPTING INSTRUCTION is the transformation of power into responsibility.*

VI. The Souls' Journey

*The thunderbolt brings rain but its lightning sets fire to the city:
The rainmaker cannot call down enough rain to keep the city from burning to the ground.*

VII. The Inertial Lines

Seven in the First Place:

*The sun focused through a magnifying glass
    ignites the dry kindling.*

One concentrated moment of spirit awakens the body.

Eight in the Second Place:

*The sun's energy passes through the food chain,
    into awareness, and back to the sun.*

The stars are angels, the galaxies archangels.

Seven in the Third Place:

*Freedom without self-discipline
    is an ordeal.*

Good fortune eludes the insincere.

Seven in the Fourth Place:

Freedom without opportunity
*   is tyranny.*

The yoke of meaningless work begs to be broken.

Eight in the Fifth Place:

Teachings devoid of ecstasy
*   do not inspire the untroubled spirit.*

Uninterrupted awe is the hallmark of authenticity.

Eight in the Sixth Place:

Teachings devoid of the numinous
*   are placebos for the troubled spirit.*

Sleepwalking through life is the hallmark of encapsulation.

SEASON 34
EVOKING OPPOSITE

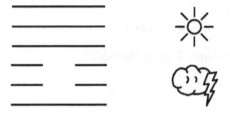

OUTER NATURE:	**SUN**
INNER NATURE:	**LIGHTNING**

I. MANTIC FORMULA

Lightning within, Sun without: The season of EVOKING OPPOSITE arrives. Success comes to those who do not relive self-defeating thoughts and memories.

Protect your spirit: The situation is one in which a clash of wills is won on the battlefield of spiritual intent.

Ally yourself with the enemy-within of your adversary: The medicine warrior lays siege to the stronghold of the enemy-within in the season of EVOKING OPPOSITE.

II. JUXTAPOSITION OF SEQUENCES

Toltec I Ching Hexagram #34
Evoking Opposite

King Wen Hexagram #34
The Power of the Great

Upper Trigram: Sun
Lower Trigram: Lightning

Upper Trigram: Lightning
Lower Trigram: Sun

III. EVOLUTION OF SEQUENCE

Sun stands in the place of Lightning above, Lightning stands in the place of Sun below: That which rises to power nurtures the enemy of its enemy.

IV. Evolution of Hexagram

Hexagram #25 Radiating Intent resolves the expanding capacity of THE POWER OF THE GREAT by returning its generative energy to widening collaboration. Sun facing Lightning was humane strength amid just movement in THE POWER OF THE GREAT—but is transformed into creative potential in the face of invigorating motivation in the season of *RADIATING INTENT*.

V. The Sequence of Seasons

Embodying the unexpected,
the true self mirrors the neutrality of nature.

After things have achieved equality, they contend for resources:
EVOKING OPPOSITE is the spiritual defense elicited by unavoidable conflict.

VI. The Souls' Journey

The rope is stretched but the knot holds:
Rebuilding the city, the traveler uncovers the city of the ancestors underneath.

VII. The Inertial Lines

Seven in the First Place:

Things that belong together
perfect one another.

Nature and human nature are twins.

Eight in the Second Place:

One's means are ennobled
by one's goal.

Pure intent transmutes the momentary into the momentous.

Eight in the Third Place:

Self-sacrifice wishes
to be shared fairly.

Ethics are divine messengers that can be called upon.

Seven in the Fourth Place:

When high hopes are rekindled
   people work unselfishly.

The monument to eternity builds itself.

Seven in the Fifth Place:

Those who have usurped the throne
   live in fear of the rightful heirs.

The powerful few dread the powerless multitude.

Seven in the Sixth Place:

Human nature cannot be changed
   by human nature.

Everything awaits the divinely inhuman.

SEASON 35
HOLDING BACK

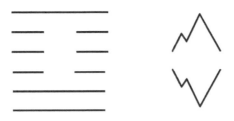

OUTER NATURE:　　MOUNTAIN
INNER NATURE:　　LAKE

I. MANTIC FORMULA

Lake within, Mountain without: The season of HOLDING BACK arrives. Success comes to those who do not act on impulse.

Your reflexes betray you: The situation is one in which one's freedom to act is voluntarily constrained.

Regret nothing, resent no one: Those who act with patience and self-awareness avoid the pitfalls of the season of HOLDING BACK.

II. JUXTAPOSITION OF SEQUENCES

Toltec I Ching Hexagram #35
Holding Back

King Wen Hexagram #35
Progress

Upper Trigram: Mountain
Lower Trigram: Lake

Upper Trigram: Fire
Lower Trigram: Moon

III. EVOLUTION OF SEQUENCE

Mountain stands in the place of Fire above, Lake stands in the place of Moon below: That which makes easy progress restrains every inclination for easy gain.

IV. Evolution of Hexagram

Hexagram #41 Feigning Compliance resolves the benevolent rulership of Progress by returning its generative energy to magnanimous liberation. Moon facing Fire was loyal devotion amid great clarity in Progress—but is transformed into realization of potential in the face of knowing judgment in the season of *Feigning Compliance.*

V. The Sequence of Seasons

Blocking others' advance,
the true self resists advancing itself.

After things have contended with injustice, they must define justice anew:
Holding Back is the instinct to transcend instinct.

VI. The Souls' Journey

The guide recovers the ancestors' artifacts:
They contain such power that the traveler must bury them again.

VII. The Inertial Lines

Seven in the First Place:

Insecurity drives troubled spirits into arenas
for which they have no calling.

Savants cultivate their utter dependence on the world soul.

Seven in the Second Place:

Evolutionary leaps are compelled
by evolutionary dead ends.

Enlightenment is an irrepressible mutation.

Eight in the Third Place:

They travel furthest
who prepare solely for the journey.

Preconceived objectives form obstacles to movement.

114

Eight in the Fourth Place:

When one's spirits are the lowest,
*   one must lift the spirits of others.*

New relationships are mutually healing.

Eight in the Fifth Place:

Those who make the most of their time in exile
*   attain greatness of spirit.*

Savants make self-cultivation their home.

Seven in the Sixth Place:

Disillusionment, when properly tempered,
*   shatters the chains.*

Suddenly freed of attachments, the soul soars.

SEASON 36
STABILIZING COMMUNION

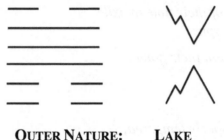

| OUTER NATURE: | LAKE |
| INNER NATURE: | MOUNTAIN |

I. MANTIC FORMULA

Mountain within, Lake without: The season of STABILIZING COMMUNION arrives. Success comes to those who immerse themselves in the sea of loving-kindness.

Melt into the-near-and-the-close: The situation is one of a self-imposed exile from the activities of society in order to commune with nature and spirit.

Embody flower-and-song: One dwells in the universal medium of belonging-together during the season of STABILIZING COMMUNION.

II. JUXTAPOSITION OF SEQUENCES

Toltec I Ching Hexagram #36
Stabilizing Communion

King Wen Hexagram #36
Darkening of the Light

Upper Trigram: Lake
Lower Trigram: Mountain

Upper Trigram: Moon
Lower Trigram: Fire

III. EVOLUTION OF SEQUENCE

Lake stands in the place of Moon above, Mountain stands in the place of Fire below: That which seeks to circumvent adversity must remain attuned to unconditional peace.

116

IV. EVOLUTION OF HEXAGRAM

Hexagram #31 Embracing Noninterference resolves the repressive adversity of DARKENING OF THE LIGHT by returning its generative energy to compassionate impartiality. Fire facing Moon was fragile light beneath dark expanse in DARKENING OF THE LIGHT—but is transformed into wisdom in the face of fulfillment in the season of *EMBRACING NONINTERFERENCE*.

V. THE SEQUENCE OF SEASONS

Preserving the valuable,
the true self dwells in blissful union with nature, spirit, and human nature.

After things are estranged, they rediscover their commonality:
STABILIZING COMMUNION is the bond of commingled energies.

VI. THE SOULS' JOURNEY

Rebuilding the city's temple, the ancestors' temple is discovered underneath:
The ancient site anchors one end of a bridge spanning time itself.

VII. THE INERTIAL LINES

Eight in the First Place:

Two mountain peaks belong together,
never touch.

What joins things is hidden deep within.

Eight in the Second Place:

Two eagles belong together,
guard their egg.

Higher and lower unite to produce the spiritual embryo.

Seven in the Third Place:

Things that belong together
remain true to their original wonder.

Transcendental recognition overwhelms the senses.

Seven in the Fourth Place:

Betrayal of trust is a hurdle to overcome,
*   not the end of the race.*

What belongs together is strengthened by crises.

Seven in the Fifth Place:

Things that belong together
*   fulfill more than themselves.*

The halo of communion expands indefinitely.

Eight in the Sixth Place:

Basing one's identity on a relationship
*   is an act of self-betrayal.*

Savants base their identity on nothing.

SEASON 37
PENETRATING CONFUSION

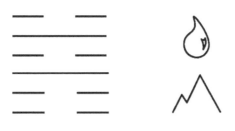

OUTER NATURE: WATER
INNER NATURE: MOUNTAIN

I. MANTIC FORMULA

Mountain within, Water without: The season of PENETRATING CONFUSION arrives. Success comes to those who cling stubbornly to the life raft of discernment.

Do not retreat from the future: The situation is one in which the illusions created by human nature fall away like scales from the eyes.

Be at peace among the night mists and the shadows: The unknown illuminates the known in the season of PENETRATING CONFUSION.

II. JUXTAPOSITION OF SEQUENCES

Toltec I Ching Hexagram #37
Penetrating Confusion

Upper Trigram: Water
Lower Trigram: Mountain

King Wen Hexagram #37
The Family [The Clan]

Upper Trigram: Wind
Lower Trigram: Fire

III. EVOLUTION OF SEQUENCE

Water stands in the place of Wind above, Mountain stands in the place of Fire below: That which holds to conventional roles and relationships eventually distinguishes between the real and illusion.

IV. EVOLUTION OF HEXAGRAM

Hexagram #39 Reviving Tradition resolves the timeworn relationships of THE FAMILY by returning its generative energy to consecrating meaningfulness. Fire facing Wind was clear order amid widespread repercussions in THE FAMILY—but is transformed into ancient wisdom in the face of adaptation to the times in the season of *REVIVING TRADITION*.

V. THE SEQUENCE OF SEASONS

At one with what is present,
the true self finds the path through the maze.

After things have shed their individuality, they lose their sense of direction:
PENETRATING CONFUSION is the loss of familiar roles and alliances.

VI. THE SOULS' JOURNEY

Ambassadors from foreign cities appear at the eastern gate:
They come seeking to make treaties with the ancestors.

VII. THE INERTIAL LINES

Eight in the First Place:

Lost in the wilderness,
one must emulate the explorer.

Everything is the path.

Eight in the Second Place:

Those who claim to know the way
do not always know the way back.

Teachers must not begin teaching too soon.

Seven in the Third Place:

Grief must pass through
authentically.

At the end of the tunnel, a new compass.

Eight in the Fourth Place:

One becomes more discerning
*   in the choice of traveling companions.*

Not all noble people share the same purpose.

Seven in the Fifth Place:

The herd
*   is a womb.*

Culture is amniotic fluid.

Eight in the Sixth Place:

The solitary horse
*   haunts the wilds.*

Savants use the empty places to fashion the world's twin.

SEASON 38
DISSOLVING ARTIFICE

OUTER NATURE: **MOUNTAIN**
INNER NATURE: **MOON**

I. MANTIC FORMULA

Moon within, Mountain without: The season of DISSOLVING ARTIFICE arrives. Success comes to those who free themselves from personal history.

Mimic the new moon: The situation is one in which efforts to regain the momentum of one's lifework are frustrated.

Sacrifice the persona: The bonds of self-image and self-interest are shattered in the season of DISSOLVING ARTIFICE.

II. JUXTAPOSITION OF SEQUENCES

Toltec I Ching Hexagram #38
Dissolving Artifice

King Wen Hexagram #38
Opposition

Upper Trigram: Mountain
Lower Trigram: Moon

Upper Trigram: Fire
Lower Trigram: Lake

III. EVOLUTION OF SEQUENCE

Mountain stands in the place of Fire above, Moon stands in the place of Lake below: That which establishes itself outside of relationships voluntarily sheds every artifice.

IV. Evolution of Hexagram

Hexagram #23 Wielding Passion resolves the diverging interests of OPPOSITION by returning its generative energy to enlivening endeavors. Lake facing Fire was fellowship with individuality in OPPOSITION—but is transformed into excitation in the face of reason in the season of *WIELDING PASSION*.

V. The Sequence of Seasons

Emptied of doubts,
the true self empties out certainties.

After things are lost, they disappear:
DISSOLVING ARTIFICE is the evaporation of conditioned identity.

VI. The Souls' Journey

The traveler is honored as the ancestors' ambassador:
The guide searches everywhere but cannot find the traveler.

VII. The Inertial Lines

Eight in the First Place:

The sculptor perfects the stone
by taking away from it.

The serpent's shed skin is key to the mysteries.

Eight in the Second Place:

Changing paths because one has been betrayed
exposes one to further disappointment.

Mosquitoes cannot bite an iron ox.

Eight in the Third Place:

Allowing oneself to be defined by others,
one becomes a stranger to oneself.

The maze of mirrors shatters before the wisdom gaze.

Eight in the Fourth Place:

Those who have perpetuated the wrongs of others
must strive tirelessly to make things right.

The universal civilizing spirit is based on self-correction.

Eight in the Fifth Place:

It is only when a community has lost its identity
that it is ready for the new.

The closer to the end, the closer to the beginning.

Seven in the Sixth Place:

The new is indelibly branded
by chance occurrences.

Mercurial spontaneity alone can adjust to the unforeseen.

SEASON 39
REVIVING TRADITION

OUTER NATURE: WIND
INNER NATURE: FIRE

I. MANTIC FORMULA

Fire within, Wind without: The season of REVIVING TRADITION arrives. Success comes to all who return to the roots of human nature.

You rejoin the children of the wind: The situation is one in which a more authentic way of life is adopted to replace one that is becoming ever less meaningful.

Seek the meaningful over the provable: The old ways are reborn to revitalize the decaying in the season of REVIVING TRADITION.

II. JUXTAPOSITION OF SEQUENCES

Toltec I Ching Hexagram #39
Reviving Tradition

Upper Trigram: Wind
Lower Trigram: Fire

King Wen Hexagram #39
Obstruction

Upper Trigram: Water
Lower Trigram: Mountain

III. EVOLUTION OF SEQUENCE

Wind stands in the place of Water above, Fire stands in the place of Mountain below: That which finds its natural course obstructed maintains its vitality in rekindled tradition.

IV. Evolution of Hexagram

Hexagram #37 Penetrating Confusion resolves the insurmountable impediments of OBSTRUCTION by returning its generative energy to the piercing of illusion. Mountain facing water was standstill amid danger in OBSTRUCTION—but is transformed into tranquil contemplation in the face of the unknown in the season of *PENETRATING CONFUSION*.

V. The Sequence of Seasons

Leaving questions and answers behind,
the true self adapts the ancient lifeway to the times.

After things have questioned their own continuity, they return to well-marked paths of conduct:
REVIVING TRADITION is the survival of meaningful form.

VI. The Souls' Journey

Treaties are made:
The traveler follows the guide, the guide follows the guardians.

VII. The Inertial Lines

Seven in the First Place:

The old ways renew
    the individual's relationship with the sacred.

Modern life is forever rooted in the ancient soul.

Eight in the Second Place:

The old ways are lost
    when people value only the visible.

Savants revere the invisible within themselves.

Seven in the Third Place:

The new temple
    is built around the old temple.

The wisdom teachings are renewed, not replaced.

Eight in the Fourth Place:

The mind measuring the footprints of spirit
*   already follows the path.*

The intellect unintentionally opens the doorway.

Seven in the Fifth Place:

The mind constantly reliving itself
*   seeks to perform an autopsy on a living body.*

The old ways have nothing to do with the past.

Seven in the Sixth Place:

The temple
*   mimics the sacred mountain.*

Savants invoke symbols to unite heaven and earth.

SEASON 40
ADAPTING EXPERIENCE

OUTER NATURE: **SUN**
INNER NATURE: **WIND**

I. MANTIC FORMULA

Wind within, Sun without: The season of ADAPTING EXPERIENCE arrives. Success comes to those who have mastered the strategies and tactics of learning.

You walk in no one's footprints: The situation is one of having accrued the judgment and tact whereby one's pursuits may continue to be cultivated despite their unconventional nature.

A measure of credibility for each measure of originality: One encounters one's historical self in the season of ADAPTING EXPERIENCE.

II. JUXTAPOSITION OF SEQUENCES

Toltec I Ching Hexagram #40
Adapting Experience

Upper Trigram: Sun
Lower Trigram: Wind

King Wen Hexagram #40
Deliverance

Upper Trigram: Lightning
Lower Trigram: Water

III. EVOLUTION OF SEQUENCE

Sun stands in the place of Lightning above, Wind stands in the place of Water below: That which is released from hardship carries true wisdom forward.

IV. Evolution of Hexagram

Hexagram #44 Refining Instinct resolves the easing tensions of Deliverance by returning its generative energy to spiritualizing desire. Water facing Lightning was danger being left behind in Deliverance — but is transformed into unfathomable mystery in the face of spiritual inspiration in the season of *Refining Instinct*.

V. The Sequence of Seasons

Carrying the ancient symbols into the present,
the true self attends to the new lessons they give life.

After things have incorporated the past, they rebuild the present:
Adapting Experience is the unearthing of an unforeseen foundation.

VI. The Souls' Journey

After five seasons, the guide discovers a secret chamber within the ancestors' temple:
A winged serpent, adorned with the sun's fire, coils dreaming upon the map of time.

VII. The Inertial Lines

Eight in the First Place:

The spirit body
  emerges from the physical cocoon.

Aware light flows forward and backward.

Seven in the Second Place:

For one, the sea is a well of tears—
  for another, it is the tide of souls.

Every symbol is a jewel of infinite facets.

Seven in the Third Place:

The arrow of longing
  pierces the thickest armor.

The greater the resistance, the deeper the barb.

Seven in the Fourth Place:

The perennial host,
*   the overnight guest.*

An idea is immortal, a thought mortal.

Seven in the Fifth Place:

A great tree
*   shelters.*

The great-souled do not hold back.

Seven in the Sixth Place:

Rainclouds gather
*   deep within the mountain.*

The spring breeze arrives from the most distant star.

SEASON 41
FEIGNING COMPLIANCE

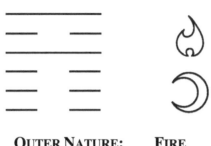

OUTER NATURE: **FIRE**
INNER NATURE: **MOON**

I. MANTIC FORMULA

Moon within, Fire without: The season of FEIGNING COMPLIANCE arrives. Success comes to those who pretend to be what they appear.

Call no attention to yourself: The situation is one of superficial conformity to enforced standards of conduct.

Do not become what you pretend to be: The indomitable soul learns to act like a contented servant in the enemy's camp during the season of FEIGNING COMPLIANCE.

II. JUXTAPOSITION OF SEQUENCES

Toltec I Ching Hexagram #41
Feigning Compliance

Upper Trigram: Fire
Lower Trigram: Moon

King Wen Hexagram #41
Decrease

Upper Trigram: Mountain
Lower Trigram: Lake

III. EVOLUTION OF SEQUENCE

Fire stands in the place of Mountain above, Moon stands in the place of Lake below: That which suffers at the hands of those above feigns docility while gathering momentum.

IV. EVOLUTION OF HEXAGRAM

Hexagram #35 Holding Back resolves the unequal allotment of DECREASE by returning its generative energy to avoiding loss. Lake facing Mountain was sacrifice amid aloofness in DECREASE—but is transformed into grateful appreciation in the face of protective restraint in the season of *HOLDING BACK*.

V. THE SEQUENCE OF SEASONS

Unfolding the ancient lessons into the future,
the true self disguises itself until the time of darkness passes.

After things have regained their stability, they begin to petrify:
FEIGNING COMPLIANCE is the hiatus between the old and the new.

VI. THE SOULS' JOURNEY

The guardians renovate the ancestors' city according to the map of time:
By the light of the smoking torch and full moon, it mirrors the heavens and the earth.

VII. THE INERTIAL LINES

Eight in the First Place:

One need not scrape barnacles from the hull
of a sinking ship.

The naive do not recognize when something has run its course.

Eight in the Second Place:

Those who wish to be deceived
will abandon one illusion only for another.

It can be dangerous to waken sleepwalkers.

Eight in the Third Place:

Those who use history to justify their actions
cannot create the future.

Visionaries are masters of the art of starting over.

Seven in the Fourth Place:

Reciprocal sacrifices
ennoble relationships.

Trust is sown in the desert and blossoms in the oasis.

Eight in the Fifth Place:

The living future inevitably embodies
the best of every culture in every time.

The sum of vision and intent equals creative power.

Seven in the Sixth Place:

The untroubled spirit has a change of heart
at the first sign of stagnation.

Loyalty to flux supersedes loyalty to comfort.

SEASON 42
INTERPRETING INSIGHT

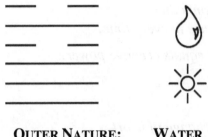

OUTER NATURE: **WATER**
INNER NATURE: **SUN**

I. MANTIC FORMULA

Sun within, Water without: The season of INTERPRETING INSIGHT arrives. Success comes to those whose thirst for light, life, liberty, and love cannot be quenched.

Reverse the mind, catapult the heart: The situation is one in which artistic expression increasingly produces works antithetical to the otherwise unchallenged indoctrination of human nature.

You master every illusion: The mirage of matter becomes the oasis of spirit in the season of INTERPRETING INSIGHT.

II. JUXTAPOSITION OF SEQUENCES

<table>
<tr><td align="center">Toltec I Ching Hexagram #42
Interpreting Insight</td><td align="center">King Wen Hexagram #42
Increase</td></tr>
<tr><td align="center"></td><td align="center"></td></tr>
<tr><td>Upper Trigram: Water
Lower Trigram: Sun</td><td>Upper Trigram: Wind
Lower Trigram: Lightning</td></tr>
</table>

III. EVOLUTION OF SEQUENCE

Water stands in the place of Wind above, Sun stands in the place of Lightning below: That which sacrifices for the sake of those below answers the call to humaneness and justice.

IV. EVOLUTION OF HEXAGRAM

Hexagram #5 Restoring Wholeness resolves the altruistic generosity of INCREASE by returning its generative energy to revitalizing well-being. Lightning facing Wind was instilling light amid dissolving shadow in INCREASE—but is transformed into evocation in the face of adaptation in the season of *RESTORING WHOLENESS*.

V. THE SEQUENCE OF SEASONS

Breaking through darkness,
the true self gives new expression to the ancient quest for perfect freedom.

After things oppress human nature, they ennoble human nature:
INTERPRETING INSIGHT is the discovery of unforeseen relationships.

VI. THE SOULS' JOURNEY

The midwife reads the map of time aloud:
An umbilical cord descends from the sky and passes through the city into the underworld.

VII. THE INERTIAL LINES

Seven in the First Place:

Awake or asleep,
*   everything dreams.*

Those who speak in dreams reach others' souls.

Seven in the Second Place:

The mind fleshes out
*   what the heart envisions.*

Recognition paves the way for interpretation.

Seven in the Third Place:

The work
*   plagiarizes itself.*

Every lifetime, every generation, truth must be retold.

Eight in the Fourth Place:

> *One remembers where one buried the treasure*
> > *last lifetime.*

> *Synchronicity, not volition, activates surviving memories.*

Seven in the Fifth Place:

> *The subjective*
> > *becomes the universal.*

> *Personal vision adds to the collective vision.*

Eight in the Sixth Place:

> *It is forever*
> > *the first glimpse.*

> *The infant's eye is wide open with wonder.*

SEASON 43
GOING BEYOND

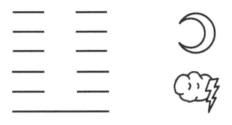

OUTER NATURE: MOON
INNER NATURE: LIGHTNING

I. MANTIC FORMULA

Lightning within, Moon without: The season of GOING BEYOND arrives. Success comes to those who break through every barrier.

You walk the sky road of stars: The situation is one in which all obstacles are overcome and all goals exceeded.

You make the beyond your home: The medicine warrior casts no shadow in the season of GOING BEYOND.

II. JUXTAPOSITION OF SEQUENCES

Toltec I Ching Hexagram #43
Going Beyond

King Wen Hexagram #43
Breakthrough [Resoluteness]

Upper Trigram: Moon
Lower Trigram: Lightning

Upper Trigram: Lake
Lower Trigram: Sun

III. EVOLUTION OF SEQUENCE

Moon stands in the place of Lake above, Lightning stands in the place of Sun below: That which removes wrongdoing transcends self-interest.

IV. EVOLUTION OF HEXAGRAM

Hexagram #24 Revealing Knowledge resolves the continuous self-examination of BREAKTHROUGH by returning its generative energy to hidden treasures. Sun facing Lake was strength with optimism in BREAKTHROUGH—but is transformed into hidden beginnings in the face of blissful awe in the season of *REVEALING* KNOWLEDGE.

V. THE SEQUENCE OF SEASONS

Giving voice to the listening heart,
the true self leaps into the bonfire of the mystical eclipse.

After things are chords of meanings, they return to silence:
GOING BEYOND is the power to move beyond the limit.

VI. THE SOULS' JOURNEY

The guide ascends the rope into the house of the sun:
The great father, the great mother, welcome their child home.

VII. THE INERTIAL LINES

Seven in the First Place:

Spirit discovers its other potential
in nature.

The spirit transcends in the body.

Eight in the Second Place:

Spawning is the hallmark
of the will to transcend.

Return to origin is the way forward.

Eight in the Third Place:

Anything, when properly tempered,
may transform into anything else.

Everything is entangled.

Eight in the Fourth Place:

In the fog, a beacon—
*   does it warn away or beckon closer?*

Savants wait as long as possible to interpret.

Eight in the Fifth Place:

Transcendence itself
*   must be transcended.*

A rope of down still binds.

Eight in the Sixth Place:

Nature transcends spirit,
*   spirit transcends nature.*

The one is manifested by the mysterious conjunction of the two.

SEASON 44
REFINING INSTINCT

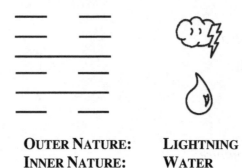

OUTER NATURE: **LIGHTNING**
INNER NATURE: **WATER**

I. MANTIC FORMULA

Water within, Lightning without: The season of REFINING INSTINCT arrives. Success comes to those who willingly redirect their instincts.

Dignify the senses, impassion the mind: The situation is one in which the pendulum has swung far enough in the direction of freedom and must be moderated before its momentum destabilizes valued roles and relationships.

Create for the future generations: The greatest monuments to the human spirit are erected in the season of REFINING INSTINCT.

II. JUXTAPOSITION OF SEQUENCES

Toltec I Ching Hexagram #44
Refining Instinct

King Wen Hexagram #44
Coming to Meet

Upper Trigram: Lightning
Lower Trigram: Water

Upper Trigram: Sun
Lower Trigram: Wind

III. EVOLUTION OF SEQUENCE

Lightning stands in the place of Sun above, Water stands in the place of Wind below: That which desires inevitably refines instinct.

IV. Evolution of Hexagram

Hexagram #40 Adapting Experience resolves the distrustful encountering of COMING TO MEET by returning its generative energy to applied learning. Wind facing Sun was entering amid strength in COMING TO MEET—but is transformed into adaptation in the face of creation in the season of *ADAPTING EXPERIENCE*.

V. The Sequence of Seasons

The true self brings the fruits of the further realms
back to the realm of the senses.

After things are elevated into a subtler form, they condense again:
REFINING INSTINCT is the practice of moving between the ethereal and the solid.

VI. The Souls' Journey

Descending and ascending, ascending and descending:
The guide rides the rainbow serpent through the three worlds.

VII. The Inertial Lines

Eight in the First Place:

Repeated shock
numbs people to shock.

Blisters become calluses.

Seven in the Second Place:

The mind cannot cradle
what the heart cannot practice.

Teachings address individual needs on the widest scale.

Eight in the Third Place:

One must further the work,
not one's own contribution.

Self-promotion is the result of insufficient training.

Seven in the Fourth Place:

Truth does not shrink when called upon
to aid its allies.

Courage in the face of intimidation averts future regret.

Eight in the Fifth Place:

Those who fear passing without leaving a trace
cannot achieve greatness.

The work is written in light, not blood.

Eight in the Sixth Place:

Those who cannot traverse the depths
do not reach the heights.

A shallow soul knows not ecstasy.

SEASON 45
CASTING OFF

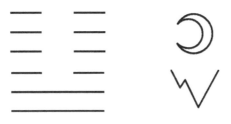

OUTER NATURE: MOON
INNER NATURE: LAKE

I. MANTIC FORMULA

Lake within, Moon without: The season of CASTING OFF arrives. Success comes to those who act with unhurried grace.

You take back your birthright: The situation is one of shedding the bonds of oppression.

The old falls away by itself: The medicine warrior dispassionately sheds the dead skin of the obsolete in the season of CASTING OFF.

II. JUXTAPOSITION OF SEQUENCES

Toltec I Ching Hexagram #45
Casting Off

Upper Trigram: Moon
Lower Trigram: Lake

King Wen Hexagram #45
Gathering Together [Massing]

Upper Trigram: Lake
Lower Trigram: Moon

III. EVOLUTION OF SEQUENCE

Moon stands in the place of Lake above, Lake stands in the place of Moon below: That which amasses for the future must cast off the past.

IV. Evolution of Hexagram

Hexagram #19 Celebrating Passage resolves the well-ordered community of GATHERING TOGETHER by returning its generative energy to commemorating transitions. Moon facing Lake was devotion amid joyousness in GATHERING TOGETHER—but is transformed into cyclic completion in the face of blessedness in the season of *CELEBRATING PASSAGE*.

V. The Sequence of Seasons

Ennobling the instincts,
the true self takes a new form.

After things have achieved true mobility, they can no longer be forced to conform:
CASTING OFF is the power to erode suffering.

VI. The Souls' Journey

The city blooms but it is not the flower the traveler planted:
The city does not become more like the traveler, but the traveler more like the city.

VII. The Inertial Lines

Seven in the First Place:

Revolutions, at every level, cannot succeed
if they fail to synchronize the old ways with the new.

The bridge of continuity spans the abyss of change.

Seven in the Second Place:

The greatest leader holds no office, wields no power,
yet leads great leaders.

True charisma endows others with new horizons.

Eight in the Third Place:

Greatness
charts its own course.

Savants live as if they were the first human being.

144

Eight in the Fourth Place:

Everything is practice
for something else.

It is a sacred game, full of momentous surprises.

Eight in the Fifth Place:

The great-souled assimilate
opposition.

Conflict is the result of short-range thinking.

Eight in the Sixth Place:

Self-imposed exile
is preferable to oppression.

Nomads simplify.

SEASON 46
HONORING CONTENTMENT

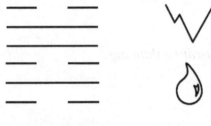

OUTER NATURE: LAKE
INNER NATURE: WATER

I. MANTIC FORMULA

Water within, Lake without: The season of HONORING CONTENTMENT arrives. Success comes to those who seek the source of serenity.

You take the path of wisdom: The situation is one in which one is content with contentment.

Your heart overflows with bliss: Well-being is transformed into wisdom and wisdom into bliss in the season of HONORING CONTENTMENT.

II. JUXTAPOSITION OF SEQUENCES

Toltec I Ching Hexagram #46
Honoring Contentment

Upper Trigram: Lake
Lower Trigram: Water

King Wen Hexagram #46
Pushing Upward

Upper Trigram: Moon
Lower Trigram: Wind

III. EVOLUTION OF SEQUENCE

Lake stands in the place of Moon above, Water stands in the place of Wind below: That which intends to reach higher must root itself in heartfelt contentment.

IV. Evolution of Hexagram

Hexagram #47 Making Individual resolves the growing advancement of Pushing Upward by returning its generative energy to crystalizing potentiality. Wind facing Moon was growth amid encouragement in Pushing Upward—but is transformed into persistent adaptation in the face of realizing potential in the season of *Making Individual*.

V. The Sequence of Seasons

Launching into new waters,
the true self treasures the joyous mystery of every moment.

After things are freed from adversity, they withdraw into happiness:
Honoring Contentment is the dwelling place of wisdom.

VI. The Souls' Journey

The traveler dwells beside the cavern's spring:
The voices of the ancestors echo day and night.

VII. The Inertial Lines

Eight in the First Place:

The closer to the light,
the greater the shadow cast.

The more joy, the more sensitive the conscience.

Seven in the Second Place:

Graduations are landmarks
on the inner ascent.

One is initiated ten thousand times a day.

Eight in the Third Place:

Those who are controlled by pleasure
no longer speak for themselves.

Wild horses do not accept bit, reins and saddle.

Seven in the Fourth Place:

Incessant worry
*   trivializes the spirit.*

The untroubled spirit turns in the direction of joy.

Seven in the Fifth Place:

Bad leaders
*   espouse progress.*

Good fortune needs no one to point it out.

Eight in the Sixth Place:

Self-righteousness
*   is self-defeating.*

To stand on tiptoe is to invite toppling.

SEASON 47
MAKING INDIVIDUAL

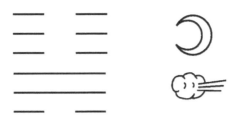

OUTER NATURE: MOON
INNER NATURE: WIND

I. MANTIC FORMULA

Wind within, Moon without: The season of MAKING INDIVIDUAL arrives. Success comes to those who seek the source of metamorphosis.

You recognize your star: The situation is one in which one embodies a new and more complete integration of human nature.

You follow your calling to the end: The historical self and the transcendental self unite in the season of MAKING INDIVIDUAL.

II. JUXTAPOSITION OF SEQUENCES

Toltec I Ching Hexagram #47
Making Individual

Upper Trigram: Moon
Lower Trigram: Wind

King Wen Hexagram #47
Oppression (Exhaustion)

Upper Trigram: Lake
Lower Trigram: Water

III. EVOLUTION OF SEQUENCE

Moon stands in the place of Lake above, Wind stands in the place of Water below: That which is emptied of opportunities rediscovers its true nature.

IV. Evolution of Hexagram

Hexagram #46 Honoring Contentment resolves the exhausted opportunities of OPPRESSION by returning its generative energy to revering blessings. Water facing Lake was danger amid carelessness in OPPRESSION—but is transformed into great mystery in the face of blissful appreciation in the season of *HONORING CONTENTMENT*.

V. The Sequence of Seasons

Abandoning all irritation,
the true self takes form in the personality.

After things have conquered unease, they spontaneously emerge in time:
MAKING INDIVIDUAL is the crystallization of the universal.

VI. The Souls' Journey

The face of the new moon, the heart of the winged serpent:
Nothing changes but the traveler becomes one of the ancestors.

VII. The Inertial Lines

Eight in the First Place:

The horse begins to anticipate
the rider's final dismount.

Awareness of mortality is physical, not mental.

Seven in the Second Place:

The smallest prism
contains the entire spectrum of light.

Focused imagination is the doorway to eternity.

Seven in the Third Place:

It is the moth who turns away from the flame
that worships the moon.

It is not given to everyone to tell the real from appearance.

150

Eight in the Fourth Place:

Water flows from its headwaters to the sea,
*   clouds flow from the sea to rain on the mountain top.*

The world soul is an alchemical retort.

Eight in the Fifth Place:

Iconoclasts become
*   the next icons.*

Polarization favors the powerful.

Eight in the Sixth Place:

Resources are limited
*   only by the social will.*

Nature's generosity must be matched by human generosity.

SEASON 48
MOVING SOURCE

OUTER NATURE: **WIND**
INNER NATURE: **WATER**

I. MANTIC FORMULA

Water within, Wind without: The season of MOVING SOURCE arrives. Success comes to those who seek the source of creativity.

You compose while performing: The situation is one of a headlong rush of events that affords no opportunity for planning or preparation.

Explore every variation on the theme: The moment-by-moment recreation of the world is exposed to view in the season of MOVING SOURCE.

II. JUXTAPOSITION OF SEQUENCES

Toltec I Ching Hexagram #48
Moving Source

King Wen Hexagram #48
The Well

Upper Trigram: Wind
Lower Trigram: Water

Upper Trigram: Water
Lower Trigram: Wind

III. EVOLUTION OF SEQUENCE

Wind stands in the place of Water above, Water stands in the place of Wind below: That which nurtures all unconditionally is embodied in the awakened heart.

IV. Evolution of Hexagram

Hexagram #59 Developing Potential resolves the inexhaustible abundance of THE WELL by returning its generative energy to creating possibilities. Wind facing Water was exhortation amid work in THE WELL— but is transformed into adaptation in the face of great mystery in the season of *DEVELOPING POTENTIAL*.

V. The Sequence of Seasons

Pivoting freely in every direction,
the true self converts poison to medicine with every encounter.

After things have fully entered history, they alter it:
MOVING SOURCE is the power to evoke unforeseen changes.

VI. The Souls' Journey

An eagle soars above the highest clouds:
The enemy-within becomes the traveler's greatest ally.

VII. The Inertial Lines

Eight in the First Place:

One becomes
> *the eye of the storm.*
All change moves on around the stillpoint.

Seven in the Second Place:

Searching for something else,
> *one finds the missing piece of the puzzle.*
Goals unintentionally serve purpose.

Eight in the Third Place:

One loses oneself
> *in every role.*
Empty going in, empty coming out.

153

Eight in the Fourth Place:

One must continually redefine the field of battle,
the rules of engagement, and the adversary.

Medicine warriors defeat that which attempts to defeat their joy of life.

Seven in the Fifth Place:

Those who continually see everything for the first time
are guided, step by step, through their lifework.

Creativity is based on receptivity.

Seven in the Sixth Place:

The window of opportunity opens,
the window of opportunity closes.

The living world responds to love.

SEASON 49
STAYING OPEN

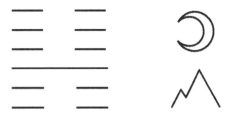

OUTER NATURE: MOON
INNER NATURE: MOUNTAIN

I. MANTIC FORMULA

Mountain within, Moon without: The season of STAYING OPEN arrives. Success comes to those who expand their vistas as wide as possible.

You do not allow yourself to be cornered: The situation is one in which a profound evolutionary leap is just beginning and has yet to be widely recognized.

You must inhabit what you build: The soul works with the coming generations in mind during the season of STAYING OPEN.

II. JUXTAPOSITION OF SEQUENCES

Toltec I Ching Hexagram #49
Staying Open

King Wen Hexagram #49
Revolution (Molting)

Upper Trigram: Moon
Lower Trigram: Mountain

Upper Trigram: Lake
Lower Trigram: Fire

III. EVOLUTION OF SEQUENCE

Moon stands in the place of Lake above, Mountain stands in the place of Fire below: That which seeks to overturn the conventional is adapting to the future.

IV. Evolution of Hexagram

Hexagram #15 Belonging Together resolves the overthrown consensus of REVOLUTION by returning its generative energy to the universal hearth. Fire facing Lake was individual clarity amid euphoric fellowship in REVOLUTION—but is transformed into understanding in the face of shared blessings in the season of *BELONGING TOGETHER*.

V. The Sequence of Seasons

Abandoning all preconceptions,
the true self explores the imaginable.

After things act with abandon, they cannot be confined in their pursuits:
STAYING OPEN is the mastery of curiosity.

VI. The Souls' Journey

From its aerie atop the sacred mountain, the eagle surveys the world:
The temple is hollow, like the cave, filled with all the treasures of time.

VII. The Inertial Lines

Eight in the First Place:

Things name themselves
to those who listen.

Savants reject the universe of words into which they are born.

Eight in the Second Place:

Sincerity without expertise may accomplish great things,
expertise without sincerity may accomplish nothing lasting.

Troubled spirits lack true concern for the consequences of their actions.

Seven in the Third Place:

Every moment is a chord
of simultaneous tones.

Harmony revolves around the root.

Eight in the Fourth Place:

*What captures and holds one's attention
        is the source of wonder.*

Openheartedness is the font of recognition.

Eight in the Fifth Place:

*Those who wander aimlessly from one interest to another
        exaggerate the value of their participation.*

Openness is based on the sense of exploration.

Eight in the Sixth Place:

*No inside
        and no outside.*

Pure awareness dwells in nonduality.

SEASON 50
NARROWING AIM

OUTER NATURE: **MOUNTAIN**
INNER NATURE: **WATER**

I. MANTIC FORMULA

Water within, Mountain without: The season of NARROWING AIM arrives. Success comes to those who focus their intent.

You find your new niche: The situation is one in which one cannot progress any further without first limiting the scope of one's endeavor.

Master your craft: The soul chips raw stone into the arrowhead's point during the season of NARROWING AIM.

II. JUXTAPOSITION OF SEQUENCES

Toltec I Ching Hexagram #50   King Wen Hexagram #50
Narrowing Aim   The Caldron

Upper Trigram: Mountain   Upper Trigram: Fire
Lower Trigram: Water   Lower Trigram: Wind

III. EVOLUTION OF SEQUENCE

Mountain stands in the place of Fire above, Water stands in the place of Wind below: That which feeds the spirit sharpens the will.

IV. EVOLUTION OF HEXAGRAM

Hexagram #4 Mirroring Wisdom resolves the nurturing fate of THE CAULDRON by returning its generative energy to mystic initiation. Wind facing Fire was the ethereal amid clarity in THE CAULDRON—but is transformed into guileless adaptation in the face of innate understanding in the season of *MIRRORING WISDOM*.

V. THE SEQUENCE OF SEASONS

*The true self funnels the possible
into concrete skills.*

*After things have been explored widely, they are explored closely:
NARROWING AIM is the mastery of detail.*

VI. THE SOULS' JOURNEY

*Of all the places in the world, the eagle chooses only this niche for its nest:
From a single stone, the mason knows the movement of the earth.*

VII. THE INERTIAL LINES

Eight in the First Place:

*Even the best-informed opinion
draws fire.*

Savants hone original thoughts.

Seven in the Second Place:

*Those who ignore details
place their endeavor at risk.*

The way forward addresses the counter-arguments.

Eight in the Third Place:

*When technicians hold sway,
one must withdraw.*

Great evil can be defeated, small-minded evil must run its course.

Eight in the Fourth Place:

Art, in any form,
*   ruptures the rational.*

The poetic genius calls forth the gods of creation.

Eight in the Fifth Place:

New information
*   improvises.*

The unprecedented creates unforeseeable relationships.

Seven in the Sixth Place:

In retrospect, one's lifework
*   appears completely premeditated.*

Only the hidden fates may wrestle dark chaos into bright order.

SEASON 51
LIVING ESSENCE

OUTER NATURE: SUN
INNER NATURE: SUN

I. MANTIC FORMULA

Sun within, Sun without: The season of LIVING ESSENCE arrives. Success comes to those who concoct the elixir of the seed.

You find the way of power: The situation is one of distilling every activity down to its original purpose.

Essence recognizes essence: By reverting to the original nature of spirit, the medicine warrior illuminates every mystery of life in the season of LIVING ESSENCE.

II. JUXTAPOSITION OF SEQUENCES

Toltec I Ching Hexagram #51
Living Essence

King Wen Hexagram #51
The Arousing (Shock, Thunder)

Upper Trigram: Sun
Lower Trigram: Sun

Upper Trigram: Lightning;
Lower Trigram: Lightning

III. EVOLUTION OF SEQUENCE

Sun stands in the place of Lightning above, Sun stands in the place of Lightning below: That which arouses reverence embodies the eternal seed.

IV. Evolution of Hexagram

Hexagram #1 Provoking Change resolves the reverential awe of THE AROUSING by returning its generative energy to breaking inertia. Lightning facing Lightning was movement upon movement in THE AROUSING—but is transformed into surprising inspiration in the face of surprising inspiration in the season of *PROVOKING CHANGE.*

V. The Sequence of Seasons

Fully prepared,
the true self steps into the secret garden of creation.

After things have been mastered, they are distilled to their fundamental nature:
LIVING ESSENCE is the invisible seed of the visible.

VI. The Souls' Journey

Two eagles mate and produce a single egg:
The soul descends from the house of the sun with a vision for the future.

VII. The Inertial Lines

Seven in the First Place:

The new must not be nurtured too little,
the new must not be protected too much.
The middle way simply avoids the extremes.

Seven in the Second Place:

One's lifelong vision
is incorruptible.
Tree rings mark the growth of the soul.

Seven in the Third Place:

Unswerving purity of intent
finds its mark.
Lightning strikes the highest summit.

162

Seven in the Fourth Place:

One foot planted firmly in the visible,
*   one foot planted firmly in the invisible.*

Wisdom is simply the absence of ignoring.

Seven in the Fifth Place:

New creations are always hybrids
*   of existing creations.*

The least likely unions produce the greatest innovations.

Seven in the Sixth Place:

The work reconciles
*   the future with the past.*

The bridge to the inevitable spans unimaginable perils.

SEASON 52
GROWING CERTAINTY

OUTER NATURE: FIRE
INNER NATURE: FIRE

I. MANTIC FORMULA

Fire within, Fire without: The season of GROWING CERTAINTY arrives. Success comes to those who do not cease questioning.

Beware self-righteousness: The situation is one of a widespread blossoming of convictions.

You tend your own hearth: Each individual's umbilical cord to spirit fans the flame of acceptance and nurturance in the season of GROWING CERTAINTY.

II. JUXTAPOSITION OF SEQUENCES

Toltec I Ching Hexagram #52
Growing Certainty

King Wen Hexagram #52
Keeping Still, Mountain

Upper Trigram: Fire
Lower Trigram: Fire

Upper Trigram: Mountain
Lower Trigram: Mountain

III. EVOLUTION OF SEQUENCE

Fire stands in the place of Mountain above, Fire stands in the place of Mountain below: That which comes to a rest attains certainty.

164

IV. EVOLUTION OF HEXAGRAM

Hexagram #30 Transforming Extinction resolves the internal stopping of KEEPING STILL by returning its generative energy to the immortal body. Mountain facing Mountain was stillness upon stillness in KEEPING STILL—but is transformed into tranquil contemplation in the face of tranquil contemplation in the season of *TRANSFORMING EXTINCTION*.

V. THE SEQUENCE OF SEASONS

The true self opens the gate
of everyday miracles.

After things have revealed their elemental nature, they act with surety:
GROWING CERTAINTY is the power of time proven exchanges.

VI. THE SOULS' JOURNEY

The hummingbird moves in the ten directions:
The map of time shows the paths and quicksand both.

VII. THE INERTIAL LINES

Seven in the First Place:

The untroubled spirit recalls things
that trouble reason.

Memories beyond the body's lifetime transform rationality.

Eight in the Second Place:

The untroubled spirit foresees things
that trouble reason.

Impressions beyond the body's senses transform rationality.

Seven in the Third Place:

The more things speed up,
the more the untroubled spirit slows down.

Change is relative.

Seven in the Fourth Place:

The troubled spirit believes it is merely
the sum of the body's experiences.

Self-interest dogs every step of the shortsighted.

Eight in the Fifth Place:

The troubled spirit cannot fashion a world view
free of contradictions.

Certainty is divisive, understanding is unifying.

Seven in the Sixth Place:

The troubled spirit cannot fashion an ethics
free of ulterior motives.

The spirit of the law suffers no loopholes.

166

SEASON 53
MASTERING REASON

OUTER NATURE: WATER
INNER NATURE: FIRE

I. MANTIC FORMULA

Fire within, Water without: The season of MASTERING REASON arrives. Success comes to those who discipline their mind.

You clear the spiderwebs from your eyes: The situation is one of setting new limits on the extent to which reason influences one's perceptions.

The winged serpent rides the breath: The medicine warrior reconciles the fire of life and water of spirit in the season of MASTERING REASON.

II. JUXTAPOSITION OF SEQUENCES

Toltec I Ching Hexagram #53   King Wen Hexagram #53
Mastering Reason   Development (Gradual Progress)

Upper Trigram: Water   Upper Trigram: Wind
Lower Trigram: Fire   Lower Trigram: Mountain

III. EVOLUTION OF SEQUENCE

Water stands in the place of Wind above, Fire stands in the place of Mountain below: That which develops at its own pace moves beyond reason.

IV. Evolution of Hexagram

Hexagram #63 Awakening Self-Sufficiency resolves the patient improvement of DEVELOPMENT by returning its generative energy to inner autonomy. Mountain facing Wind was abiding in dignity amid positive influence in DEVELOPMENT—but is transformed into stability in the face of adaptation in the season of *AWAKENING SELF-SUFFICIENCY*.

V. The Sequence of Seasons

Unleashing the floodtide of metamorphosis,
the true self navigates the laws of spiritual cause-and-effect.

After things are known to be true, they proceed according to fixed laws:
MASTERING REASON is the extension of the known into the unknown.

VI. The Souls' Journey

The midwife readies the steam bath and conducts the cleansing ritual:
The marriage of fire and water gives birth to the diamond body.

VII. The Inertial Lines

Seven in the First Place:

Reason knows only what the senses
decide it should know.

Mites know a small universe.

Eight in the Second Place:

Reason is predisposed
to confirming preconceptions.
Novelty demands adaptation to change.

Seven in the Third Place:

Reason is predisposed
to identifying with what it thinks.

Mirrors are not the reflections they hold.

Eight in the Fourth Place:

Reason is easily convinced
but difficult to change.

Conversion reaches into levels deeper than thinking.

Seven in the Fifth Place:

Reason is predisposed
to intervening in the natural course of events.

Nature evolved reason for defense, not competition.

Eight in the Sixth Place:

Reason is not predisposed
to refraining from thinking.

A statue faces a book of painted birds.

SEASON 54
REPEATING TEST

OUTER NATURE:	**SUN**
INNER NATURE:	**MOON**

I. MANTIC FORMULA

Moon within, Sun without: The season of REPEATING TEST arrives. Success comes to those who heal the past.

Seize your second chance: The situation is one of repeating a past challenge as one would have originally wished.

Go backwards in order to advance: One steps behind one's own shadow in order to erase all regrets during the season of REPEATING TEST.

II. JUXTAPOSITION OF SEQUENCES

<table>
<tr><td>Toltec I Ching Hexagram #54
Repeating Test</td><td>King Wen Hexagram #54
The Marrying Maiden</td></tr>
<tr><td>Upper Trigram: Sun
Lower Trigram: Moon</td><td>Upper Trigram: Lightning
Lower Trigram: Lake</td></tr>
</table>

III. EVOLUTION OF SEQUENCE

Sun stands in the place of Lightning above, Moon stands in the place of Lake below: That which makes decisions based on affinity regains past momentum.

170

IV. Evolution of Hexagram

Hexagram #12 Seeing Ahead resolves the impulsive union of THE MARRYING MAIDEN by returning its generative energy to foreseeing destiny. Lake facing Lightning was joyousness amid movement in THE MARRYING MAIDEN—but is transformed into mystical wonder in the face of an inspiring breakthrough in the season of *SEEING AHEAD*.

V. The Sequence of Seasons

The true self places effect before cause
within the inner time of soul-making.

After things have revealed their natural order, they turn back in upon themselves:
REPEATING TEST is the retying of the knot of fate.

VI. The Souls' Journey

The midday sun absorbs the full moon:
In the living midnight of the eclipse's shadow, the city shines like the sun.

VII. The Inertial Lines

Eight in the First Place:

Outside the body
        another body.

The spirit body transforms constantly.

Eight in the Second Place:

Within the mind
        another mind.

The groundwater of being surfaces in each well of thinking.

Eight in the Third Place:

The butterfly
        reenters the cocoon.

Cultivation completes awakening.

171

Seven in the Fourth Place:

> *Flowers sing,*
> > *songs blossom.*
>
> *Savants develop other senses.*

Seven in the Fifth Place:

> *The recurring nightmare*
> > *ends.*
>
> *Character is freedom.*

Seven in the Sixth Place:

> *Cataclysmic change*
> > *is not inevitable.*
>
> *The world soul gives birth to the universal civilizing spirit.*

SEASON 55
INTERNALIZING PURITY

OUTER NATURE: SUN
INNER NATURE: MOUNTAIN

I. MANTIC FORMULA

Mountain within, Sun without: The season of INTERNALIZING PURITY arrives. Success comes to those who stand against the tide of intolerance.

Holding your ground leads to victory: The situation is one in which the mounting demands for conformity are masked as a movement of social reform.

You have no hunger in your spirit: All the adversary's strategies of subliminal conquest are exposed to view in the season of INTERNALIZING PURITY.

II. JUXTAPOSITION OF SEQUENCES

Toltec I Ching Hexagram #55
Internalizing Purity

King Wen Hexagram #55
Abundance [Fullness]

Upper Trigram: Sun
Lower Trigram: Mountain

Upper Trigram: Lightning
Lower Trigram: Fire

III. EVOLUTION OF SEQUENCE

Sun stands in the place of Lightning above, Mountain stands in the place of Fire below: That which reaches fullness empties the heart of all but goodwill.

IV. Evolution of Hexagram

Hexagram #33 Accepting Instruction resolves the fortuitous circumstances of ABUNDANCE by returning its generative energy to open-hearted sincerity. Fire facing Lightning was clarity amid progress in ABUNDANCE—but is transformed into knowledge in the face of motivation in the season of *ACCEPTING INSTRUCTION*.

V. The Sequence of Seasons

The old dam broken open,
the true self surges toward the sea of light.

After things reconcile the past with the present, they reconcile the present with the future:
INTERNALIZING PURITY is the untying of the knot of fate.

VI. The Souls' Journey

Within the temple, the golden sun shines:
Within the traveler, the temple stands dark and still.

VII. The Inertial Lines

Eight in the First Place:

One becomes
the lunar jaguar.
In the dark of night, all distinctions run together.

Eight in the Second Place:

One becomes
the solar eagle.
In the light of day, all discernments evoke meaning.

Seven in the Third Place:

Self-sacrifice
should remain anonymous.
Desire for recognition makes a lie of truth.

174

Seven in the Fourth Place:

The axolotl
>   *bides its time.*

Adult behaviors are learned, not innate.

Seven in the Fifth Place:

The ship
>   *casts loose its anchor.*

The music of spirit carries all away.

Seven in the Sixth Place:

Lightning and thunder
>   *arrive as one.*

Not a hair's breadth between the world soul and the soul.

SEASON 56
RECAPTURING VISION

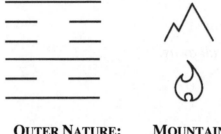

OUTER NATURE:	MOUNTAIN
INNER NATURE:	FIRE

I. MANTIC FORMULA

Fire within, Mountain without: The season of RECAPTURING VISION arrives. Success comes to all who have safeguarded their dreams.

You disavow every compromise: The situation is one of reawakened idealism.

Promise overturns every obstacle: Welling up from its very core, the world of dreaming irrupts into the world of waking in the season of RECAPTURING VISION.

II. JUXTAPOSITION OF SEQUENCES

Toltec I Ching Hexagram #56
Recapturing Vision

Upper Trigram: Mountain
Lower Trigram: Fire

King Wen Hexagram #56
The Wanderer

Upper Trigram: Fire
Lower Trigram: Mountain

III. EVOLUTION OF SEQUENCE

Mountain stands in the place of Fire above, Fire stands in the place of Mountain below: That which does not abide does not lose sight of the ideal.

IV. EVOLUTION OF HEXAGRAM

Hexagram #22 Sharing Memory resolves the accommodating transience of THE WANDERER by returning its generative energy to the collective memory. Mountain facing Fire was inner reserve with clarity in THE WANDERER—but is transformed into tranquil contemplation in the face of true knowing in the season of *SHARING MEMORY*.

V. THE SEQUENCE OF SEASONS

Seeing through every pretense of progress,
the true self holds the ancient quest sacred.

After things have protected the real, they evoke the ideal:
RECAPTURING VISION is the challenging of new meanings by the old.

VI. THE SOULS' JOURNEY

The temple fire is extinguished and then rekindled:
Sacred vessels and monuments are broken and new ones take their place.

VII. THE INERTIAL LINES

Seven in the First Place:

Anonymous power
dehumanizes.

When everyone is infected, it is no longer called an illness.

Eight in the Second Place:

Differences are cultivated
to keep the community from uniting.

The middle is a vacuum once everyone is at extremes.

Seven in the Third Place:

The great-souled are not alienated
from their contemporaries.

Savants are ordinary people who have completed their work.

Eight in the Fourth Place:

Time sanctifies
one's dream.

The seed vision becomes a forest shared by many.

Eight in the Fifth Place:

Selfsameness is cultivated
to unite with other traditions.

Before differences, all walk the same path.

Seven in the Sixth Place:

The great-souled hold sacred
the beliefs of others.

After differences, all walk the same path.

SEASON 57
DEFYING UNCERTAINTY

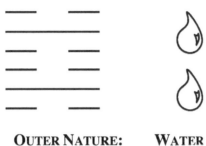

OUTER NATURE: **WATER**
INNER NATURE: **WATER**

I. Mantic Formula

Water within, Water without: The season of DEFYING UNCERTAINTY arrives. Success comes to those who dwell in the heart of peace.

You allow change to pass through you: The situation is one of having to confront an unexpected crisis of faith.

The forest mimics the chameleon: The soul extinguishes every thought that seeks to extinguish the perfection of the present moment in the season of DEFYING UNCERTAINTY.

II. JUXTAPOSITION OF SEQUENCES

Toltec I Ching Hexagram #57
Defying Uncertainty

Upper Trigram: Water
Lower Trigram: Water

King Wen Hexagram #57
The Gentle (The Penetrating, Wind)

Upper Trigram: Wind
Lower Trigram: Wind

III. EVOLUTION OF SEQUENCE

Water stands in the place of Wind above, Water stands in the place of Wind below: That which penetrates to the heart of things is not disheartened by uncertainty.

179

IV. EVOLUTION OF HEXAGRAM

Hexagram #29 Sustaining Resilience resolves the constant purposefulness of THE GENTLE by returning its generative energy to unrelenting flexibility. Wind facing Wind was dispersing resistances amid accomplishing undertakings in THE GENTLE—but is transformed into spontaneous adaptation in the face of unpredictable adaptation in the season of *SUSTAINING RESILIENCE*.

V. THE SEQUENCE OF SEASONS

Keeping to the path of freedom,
the true self passes unscathed through the mire of fate.

After things aspire to the true, they enter the maze of questions:
DEFYING UNCERTAINTY is the transformative power of the unforeseeable.

VI. THE SOULS' JOURNEY

The city is enveloped in night mists:
Ominous forms wander the deserted streets and the sounds of dice echo in the mist.

VII. THE INERTIAL LINES

Eight in the First Place:

Trepidation
        brings trepidation.

Anxiety is mistaken for excitement.

Seven in the Second Place:

Repeated unpredictable change
        brings predictable change.

When the senses are overwhelmed, reactions grow dulled.

Eight in the Third Place:

One person allied with chance
        changes the momentum.

Spontaneous random behavior is difficult to achieve.

Eight in the Fourth Place:

Chance events, when properly pursued,
* lead to the heart's desire.*

Spontaneous random events are difficult to employ.

Seven in the Fifth Place:

The work
* kills death.*

At the bottom of the abyss, the river of life.

Eight in the Sixth Place:

Unavoidable catastrophe
* is averted.*

Wisdom prevails when all else fails.

SEASON 58
DAWNING EXISTENCE

OUTER NATURE: **MOON**
INNER NATURE: **MOON**

I. MANTIC FORMULA

Moon within, Moon without: The season of DAWNING EXISTENCE arrives. Success comes to all.

The trials are all passed: The situation is one of reaching the destination.

You dwell in the primordial home: The medicine warrior's work embraces the first ancestor's every creation in the season of DAWNING EXISTENCE.

II. JUXTAPOSITION OF SEQUENCES

Toltec I Ching Hexagram #58
Dawning Existence

King Wen Hexagram #58
The Joyous, Lake

Upper Trigram: Moon
Lower Trigram: Moon

Upper Trigram: Lake
Lower Trigram: Lake

III. EVOLUTION OF SEQUENCE

Moon stands in the place of Lake above, Moon stands in the place of Lake below: That which rejoices embodies ever-dawning existence.

182

IV. Evolution of Hexagram

Hexagram #2 Sensing Creation resolves the sober elation of THE JOYOUS by returning its generative energy to all-embracing reconciliation. Lake facing Lake was rejoicing upon rejoicing in THE JOYOUS — but is transformed into mystical wonder in the face of mystical wonder in the season of *SENSING* CREATION.

V. The Sequence of Seasons

Perfected by ordeal,
the true self manifests as crystalized idea.

After things turn inward, they turn outward:
DAWNING EXISTENCE is the ground of unforeseen becoming.

VI. The Souls' Journey

An owl glides silent as midnight in the forest:
The midwife descends from the house of the moon with music and medicine.

VII. The Inertial Lines

Eight in the First Place:

The greater the pressure,
the more perfect the diamond.

Concentration crystalizes intent.

Eight in the Second Place:

The greater the need,
the stronger the medicine.

Benefit comprises equal parts compassion and wisdom.

Eight in the Third Place:

The greater the contribution,
the wider the reception.

All the land awaits the rain with open arms.

Eight in the Fourth Place:

The greater the vision,
the higher the duties.

Archangels care for angels, angels care for people, people care for the earth.

Eight in the Fifth Place:

The greater the self-discipline,
the purer the freedom.

The path grows wider as it grows longer.

Eight in the Sixth Place:

The greater the victory,
the easier the surrender.

When there is nothing left to lose, victory is complete.

SEASON 59
DEVELOPING POTENTIAL

OUTER NATURE: WATER
INNER NATURE: WIND

I. MANTIC FORMULA

Wind within, Water without: The season of DEVELOPING POTENTIAL arrives. Success comes to those who perceive the promise of further transformation.

You rewrite your future: The situation is one of creating new possibilities.

Nothing will be left undone: The soul sows the seeds of future metamorphosis in the season of DEVELOPING POTENTIAL.

II. JUXTAPOSITION OF SEQUENCES

Toltec I Ching Hexagram #59
Developing Potential

King Wen Hexagram #59
Dispersion [Dissolution]

Upper Trigram: Water
Lower Trigram: Wind

Upper Trigram: Wind
Lower Trigram: Water

III. EVOLUTION OF SEQUENCE

Water stands in the place of Wind above, Wind stands in the place of Water below: That which dissolves rigidity creates possibilities.

IV. EVOLUTION OF HEXAGRAM

Hexagram #48 Moving Source resolves the disunity overcome of DISPERSION by returning its generative energy to the living path. Water facing Wind was the dark amid the breaking up and dissolving of shadow in DISPERSION—but is transformed into unfathomable mystery in the face of unpredictable adaptation in the season of *MOVING SOURCE*.

V. THE SEQUENCE OF SEASONS

Drawing from the inner well of finishing,
the true self pours attention onto outer seeds.

After things have been exposed to the elements, they waken the dormant seed:
DEVELOPING POTENTIAL is the power of the dream.

VI. THE SOULS' JOURNEY

The wind clears away the mists from the city:
From atop the temple, the traveler can see forever.

VII. THE INERTIAL LINES

Eight in the First Place:

Dreams speak
        in the language of reuniting.

Symbols draw mortal emotion and immortal meaning together.

Seven in the Second Place:

Dreams mislead the rational mind
        in order to guide the heart.

Reason ignores the straight path to the center of the maze.

Seven in the Third Place:

Dreams are the wellspring
        of each moment's least likely possibility.

Creativity drinks from the font of meaningful coincidences.

186

Eight in the Fourth Place:

The parallel life of the dream body is forgotten
*   until one is strong enough to live it.*

Only the fully awake walk both realms at the same time.

Seven in the Fifth Place:

The dream body awakens
*   in the full light of day.*

All at once, everything in the universe sheds its dead skin.

Eight in the Sixth Place:

Little by little, the dream body stretches
*   the umbilical cord in every direction.*

From the moment it is birthed, the new immortal strives to explore.

SEASON 60
CHANGING ALLIANCES

OUTER NATURE: **WIND**
INNER NATURE: **MOON**

I. MANTIC FORMULA

Moon within, Wind without: The season of CHANGING ALLIANCES arrives. Success comes to those who maintain a continuity of values in the midst of change.

End things well: The situation is one of creating new alliances.

Think spiritually but act politically: The soul acts with the purest intentions and the subtlest diplomacy in the season of CHANGING ALLIANCES.

II. JUXTAPOSITION OF SEQUENCES

Toltec I Ching Hexagram #60
Changing Alliances

Upper Trigram: Wind
Lower Trigram: Moon

King Wen Hexagram #60
Limitation

Upper Trigram: Water
Lower Trigram: Lake

III. EVOLUTION OF SEQUENCE

Wind stands in the place of Water above, Moon stands in the place of Lake below: That which has limits changes associations.

IV. EVOLUTION OF HEXAGRAM

Hexagram #20 Entering Service resolves the responsible bounds of LIMITATION by returning its generative energy to selfless healing. Lake facing Water was joyousness amid danger in LIMITATION—but is transformed into sharing blessings in the face of secret work in the season of *ENTERING SERVICE*.

V. THE SEQUENCE OF SEASONS

Exposing new opportunities,
the true self pursues new relationships.

After things have waited to come into the world, they unleash the whirlwind:
CHANGING ALLIANCES is the unforeseen reunion of kindred dreamers.

VI. THE SOULS' JOURNEY

A new world tree sprouts from the underworld and pierces the sky in a single day:
The guide returns from the other side with gold and silver, turquoise and obsidian.

VII. THE INERTIAL LINES

Eight in the First Place:

Metamorphosis
comes full circle.

The possibility of parting causes things to change back.

Eight in the Second Place:

Every blossom
offers nectar.

It is the music, not the musician, that entrances.

Eight in the Third Place:

Great companions
offer great solitude.

Half the lessons on the road are personal.

Eight in the Fourth Place:

Troubled spirits
*   attract troubled spirits.*

Two half persons do not make a whole relationship.

Seven in the Fifth Place:

One's lifework dissolves
*   into the anonymity of the work.*

It is the bonfire, not the firewood, that rends the dark.

Seven in the Sixth Place:

The work
*   is a cocoon.*

Those who do not identify with the body change form.

SEASON 61
STRENGTHENING INTEGRITY

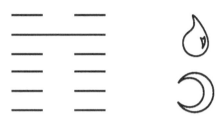

OUTER NATURE: **WATER**
INNER NATURE: **MOON**

I. MANTIC FORMULA

Moon within, Water without: The season of STRENGTHENING INTEGRITY arrives. Success comes to those who grow weary of being at the mercy of their weaknesses.

You embody the first person: The situation is one of creating new instincts.

Train one another: Inspired by the accomplishments of their predecessors, a new generation of souls is born in the season of STRENGTHENING INTEGRITY.

II. JUXTAPOSITION OF SEQUENCES

Toltec I Ching Hexagram #61
Strengthening Integrity

Upper Trigram: Water
Lower Trigram: Moon

King Wen Hexagram #61
Inner Truth

Upper Trigram: Wind
Lower Trigram: Lake

III. EVOLUTION OF SEQUENCE

Water stands in the place of Wind above, Moon stands in the place of Lake below: That which attains authenticity complements solidarity.

IV. Evolution of Hexagram

Hexagram #8 Harmonizing Duality resolves the sympathetic appreciation of INNER TRUTH by returning its generative energy to balancing halves. Lake facing Wind was joyousness amid gentleness in INNER TRUTH—but is transformed into wonder in the face of adaptation in the season of *HARMONIZING DUALITY*.

V. The Sequence of Seasons

Forming new bonds,
the true self exemplifies the spirit of mutual cultivation.

After things have found their new place in the whole, they take root:
STRENGTHENING INTEGRITY is the concretization of the dream.

VI. The Souls' Journey

The traveler leaves behind footprints of silver and gold, turquoise and obsidian:
The city stands perfected, glistening in the dew.

VII. The Inertial Lines

Eight in the First Place:

Familiarity
breeds indivisibility.

The roots of trees intertwine.

Eight in the Second Place:

The great-souled take nothing
for granted.

Every moment is an abyss filled with awe.

Eight in the Third Place:

Those who exploit others
torture their own soul.

Hunger does not gnaw at the satisfied.

Eight in the Fourth Place:

> *The perennial truth*
> > *is ecstatic.*
>
> *Everything already exists and cannot be destroyed.*

Seven in the Fifth Place:

> *The great-souled*
> > *empower.*
>
> *Magnanimous intent fortifies and launches.*

Eight in the Sixth Place:

> *Time*
> > *grieves.*
>
> *The present honors the past with living tears.*

SEASON 62
CONCEIVING SPIRIT

OUTER NATURE: SUN
INNER NATURE: FIRE

I. MANTIC FORMULA

Fire within, Sun without: The season of CONCEIVING SPIRIT arrives. Success comes to those who grow weary of the limits of their awareness.

You open the other eye: The situation is one of creating new perceptions.

Time is your ally: The soul turns attention itself around in order to see awareness as it truly is in the season of CONCEIVING SPIRIT.

II. JUXTAPOSITION OF SEQUENCES

Toltec I Ching Hexagram #62
Conceiving Spirit

Upper Trigram: Sun
Lower Trigram: Fire

King Wen Hexagram #62
Preponderance of the Small

Upper Trigram: Lightning
Lower Trigram: Mountain

III. EVOLUTION OF SEQUENCE

Sun stands in the place of Lightning above, Fire stands in the place of Mountain below: That which exits the maze of fate enters the realm of immortality.

IV. EVOLUTION OF HEXAGRAM

Hexagram #13 Concentrating Attention resolves the dutiful judiciousness of PREPONDERANCE OF THE SMALL by returning its generative energy to immediate single-mindedness. Mountain facing Lightning was limitation amid movement in PREPONDERANCE OF THE SMALL—but is transformed into tranquil contemplation in the face of consistent motivation in the season of *CONCENTRATING ATTENTION*.

V. THE SEQUENCE OF SEASONS

The work of union completed,
the true self brings to light the dream body of metamorphosis.

After things act without forethought, they perceive the dreaming world:
CONCEIVING SPIRIT is the unforeseen experience of the forces radiating the visible.

VI. THE SOULS' JOURNEY

The wheel of light turns on its hidden axis:
Rising and falling, the currents of the sun and moon course through the jade heart.

VII. THE INERTIAL LINES

Seven in the First Place:

The undisciplined mind is quick to assume
that everything invisible is of its making.

One's own invisible half communes with the invisible half of all.

Eight in the Second Place:

The disciplined mind conceives
what the senses cannot perceive.

Focused imagination re-enters the world soul.

Seven in the Third Place:

Ulterior motives
corrupt intention.

Pure intention divests itself of self-interest.

Seven in the Fourth Place:

Emotions come from the outside
and return to the outside.

The gods and goddesses are immortal and impersonal.

Seven in the Fifth Place:

One's spirit reflects
the spirit of nature.

Everything is a distinct idea within the one mind.

Seven in the Sixth Place:

One's stone is set into the base
of the pyramid.

One's lifework is foundational.

SEASON 63
AWAKENING SELF-SUFFICIENCY

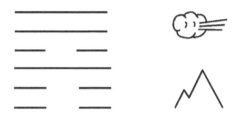

OUTER NATURE: **WIND**
INNER NATURE: **MOUNTAIN**

I. MANTIC FORMULA

Mountain within, Wind without: The season of AWAKENING SELF-SUFFICIENCY arrives. Success comes to those who keep the open secret.

You fashion your mask from a mirror: The situation is one of mastering the awakened way of life.

The way of the vulture is the path of self-sustaining wisdom: The medicine warrior creates well-being by transforming the most common grain of sand into a hidden pearl during the season of AWAKENING SELF-SUFFICIENCY.

II. JUXTAPOSITION OF SEQUENCES

Toltec I Ching Hexagram #63
Awakening Self-Sufficiency

King Wen Hexagram #63
After Completion

Upper Trigram: Wind
Lower Trigram: Mountain

Upper Trigram: Water
Lower Trigram: Fire

III. EVOLUTION OF SEQUENCE

Wind stands in the place of Water above, Mountain stands in the place of Fire below: That which completes its purpose attains self-sufficiency.

IV. EVOLUTION OF HEXAGRAM

Hexagram #53 Mastering Reason resolves the insightful precautions of AFTER COMPLETION by returning its generative energy to divine intelligence. Fire facing Water was foresight amid danger in AFTER COMPLETION—but is transformed into wisdom in the face of unfathomable mystery in the season of *MASTERING REASON*.

V. THE SEQUENCE OF SEASONS

Cutting the umbilical cord,
the true self joins forces with the dream bodies of others.

After things are no longer disguised, they become a disguise:
AWAKENING SELF-SUFFICIENCY is the acceptance of the force radiating oneself.

VI. THE SOULS' JOURNEY

The pupil of the eye, the dark mirror of time:
The winged serpent awakens and departs the temple.

VII. THE INERTIAL LINES

Eight in the First Place:

One becomes
one of the ancestors.

Savants experience death of the ego while the body lives.

Eight in the Second Place:

Those who cannot be content with the necessities of life
hold others hostage.

Nothing is better than a world of universal happiness.

Seven in the Third Place:

Each new generation
returns to the old ways.

History inevitably embodies the universal civilizing spirit.

198

Eight in the Fourth Place:

One becomes
the land.

Identity inevitably embodies the love of creation.

Seven in the Fifth Place:

Those who do not meet their fate with dignity and courage
betray themselves at the end.

The great-hearted leap ecstatically from lifetime to lifetime.

Seven in the Sixth Place:

Spirit, and spirit alone,
escapes erosion.

Only the unchanging passes unscathed through the world of change.

SEASON 64
SAFEGUARDING LIFE

OUTER NATURE: **MOUNTAIN**
INNER NATURE: **WIND**

I. MANTIC FORMULA

Wind within, Mountain without: The season of SAFEGUARDING LIFE arrives. Success comes to those who live within their means.

You balance the scales: The situation is one of honoring that upon which all depend.

Win hearts, not minds: Because the sacred war can be won only through self-sacrifice, the medicine warrior reflects only love for the life-giving forces in the season of SAFEGUARDING LIFE.

II. JUXTAPOSITION OF SEQUENCES

Toltec I Ching Hexagram #64
Safeguarding Life

King Wen Hexagram #64
Before Completion

Upper Trigram: Mountain
Lower Trigram: Wind

Upper Trigram: Fire
Lower Trigram: Water

III. EVOLUTION OF SEQUENCE

Mountain stands in the place of Fire above, Wind stands in the place of Water below: That which paves the way for order out of confusion safeguards the irreplaceable.

IV. Evolution of Hexagram

Hexagram #18 Resolving Paradox resolves the preparatory transition of BEFORE COMPLETION by returning its generative energy to marrying opposites. Water facing Fire was work amid foresight in BEFORE COMPLETION—but is transformed into unfathomable mystery in the face of understanding in the season of *RESOLVING PARADOX*.

V. The Sequence of Seasons

The tide of dreams turning,
the true self stands against the nightmare.

After things are treasured for themselves, they become allies:
SAFEGUARDING LIFE is the marshaling of movement into the inevitable direction.

VI. The Souls' Journey

Religion and science, art and magic:
The traveler and the guide return to the road, carrying the city with them.

VII. The Inertial Lines

Eight in the First Place:

Nature takes root
in one's dreams.

The world soul cries out.

Seven in the Second Place:

Those who do not honor the ancestors
have no lineage.

In a sea of spirit, all lifetimes are fused as one.

Seven in the Third Place:

A city with no conscience
is a ghost town.

The living community is guided by vision, care and renewal.

Eight in the Fourth Place:

>   *One's dreams take root*
>   >   *in nature.*

>   *One's soul restores the balance.*

Eight in the Fifth Place:

>   *Those who do not honor the descendants*
>   >   *bow to self-defeat.*

>   *The heirloom must enrich, not burden.*

Seven in the Sixth Place:

>   *The spirit within the stone*
>   >   *crowns the temple.*

>   *Innate perfectibility seals humanity's destiny.*

APPENDIX

THE COIN METHOD OF CONSULTING THE ORACLE

The coin oracle consists of six throws of three coins.
Each throw signifies one of the six lines of a hexagram.
Heads have an assigned value of 3. Tails have an assigned value of 2.
Since each throw uses three coins, only four possible results can be obtained for each line:

Three Tails =	$2 + 2 + 2 = 6$
Two Tails & One Heads =	$2 + 2 + 3 = 7$
Two Heads & One Tails =	$3 + 3 + 2 = 8$
Three Heads =	$3 + 3 + 3 = 9$

Being more balanced between both sides of the coins, the totals 7 and 8 were assigned a static nature of solid and broken lines:

$7 =$ ———————— $8 =$ —— ——

Being over-balanced on one side of the coins, the totals 6 and 9 were assigned a changing nature of changing broken and changing solid lines:

$6 =$ ——x—— $9 =$ ——⊖——

Because there are only two types of lines—solid and broken—changing broken lines change into solid lines and vice versa: a six, having come to its extreme, changes into its opposite, a seven and, likewise, a nine, having reached its extreme, changes into its opposite, an eight.

——x—— —> ———————— (6 changing to a seven)
——⊖—— —> —— —— (9 changing to an eight)

To begin with, each of the 64 hexagrams consists of six horizontal lines stacked vertically—**the bottom line being the first and the top line the sixth**. Furthermore, each line can embody one of four qualities: (1) a solid line; (2) a broken line; (3) a solid line changing into a broken line; and, (4) a broken line changing into a solid line. And, finally, when lines of a hexagram change, that hexagram changes into another hexagram.

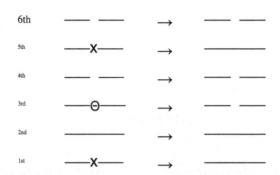

Examining the hexagram on the left in the example above, we can see that the 2nd, 4th, and 6th lines are unchanging: the 2nd is a solid line, while the 4th and 6th are broken lines. Likewise, we can see that in that same hexagram the 1st, 3rd, and 5th lines are changing into their opposite qualities: the 1st is a broken line changing into a solid line, the 3rd is a solid line changing into a broken line, and the 5th is a broken line changing into a solid line.

When each of the lines in the hexagram on the left is carried forward, the second hexagram on the right is formed. The broken line in the 1st place changes into the broken line in the 1st place of the hexagram on the right. The solid line in the 2nd place is unchanging, so it is carried forward as a solid line in the 2nd place of the hexagram on the right. The solid line in the 3rd place changes into the broken line in the 3rd place of the hexagram on the right. The broken line in the 4th place is unchanging, so it is carried forward as a broken line in the 4th place of the hexagram on the right. The broken line in the 5th place changes into a solid line in the 5th place of the hexagram on the right. The broken line in the 6th place is unchanging, so it is carried forward as a broken line in the 6th place of the hexagram on the right. *This methodology whereby hexagrams transform into one another is the key factor whereby the I Ching exposes the development of the present situation into the future situation.*

It is important to note that some readings result in *six unchanging lines*, in which case the reading consists of one hexagram, rather than two. This generally implies a relatively stable situation that is evolving in accord with the flow of the hexagrams in the sequence (e.g., Hexagram #35 would be evolving into Hexagram #36, Hexagram #54 into Hexagram #55, etc.).

Once these two hexagrams (or one hexagram, if there are no line changes) have been determined, identify their hexagram numbers by means of the chart on the next page and then consult the respective texts in *The Toltec I Ching*.

HEXAGRAM IDENTIFICATION CHART

Upper→ / Lower↓	☷	☶	☵	☳	☴	☲	☱	☷
	2	23	8	45	16	12	20	35
	15	52	39	31	62	33	53	56
	7	4	29	47	40	6	59	64
	19	41	60	58	54	10	61	38
	24	27	3	17	51	25	42	21
	11	26	5	43	34	1	9	14
	46	18	48	28	32	44	57	50
	36	22	63	49	55	13	37	30

Locate the Hexagram Number at the intersection of the Upper and Lower Trigrams

3 + 4 :: 6 + 1 :: RETURN

The Toltec I Ching
        with Martha Ramirez-Oropeza
In the Oneness of Time: The Education of a Diviner
Way of the Diviner
When You Catch the Fish, Throw Away the Net: An Autobibliography
The Divine Dark: Mystery as Origin and Destination
In Search of the Inevitable: Signatures of Celestial Divination
The Oracle Whispers: Echoes from the Edge of Creation

RESEARCHES ON THE TOLTEC I CHING:

Vol. 1. *I Ching Mathematics: The Science of Change*
Vol. 2. *The Image and Number Treatise: The Oracle and the War on Fate*
Vol. 3. *The Forest of Fire Pearls Oracle: The Medicine Warrior I Ching*
Vol. 4. *I Ching Mathematics for the King Wen Version*
Vol. 5. *Why Study the I Ching: A Brief Course in the Direct Seeing of Reality*
Vol. 6. *The Open Secret I Ching: The Diviner's Journey and the Road of Freedom*
Vol. 7. *The Alchemical I Ching: 64 Keys to the Secret of Internal Transmutation*
Vol. 8. *intrachange: I Ching Chess*
Vol. 9. *The Before Heaven I Ching: Reading the Text of Creation*
Vol. 10. *I Ching Talismans: Forge of Spiritual Sigils*

SELF-REALIZATION PRACTICES:

The Five Emanations: Aligning the Modern Mind with the Ancient Soul
The Spiritual Basis of Good Fortune: Retracing the Ancient Path of Personal Transformation
Facing Light: Preparing for the Moment of Dying
The Art of Divination: The Role of Consciousness and Will in Stepping Outside Time

POETRY:

Palimpsest Flesh
Fragments of Anamnesia
The Soul of Power: Deconstructing the Art of War
The Tao of Cool: Deconstructing the Tao Te Ching
We Are I Am: Visions of Mystical Union

NOVEL:

Life and Death in the Hotel Bardo